To The President

The Victoria Cross a

Association.

With humble respects.

Mann Bainsfeed.

15 May 1986.

'GAINST ALL DISASTER

The group of decorations and medals awarded to
Group Captain O. C. Bryson, RAF, late RFC and Dorset Yeomanry.
Note the unusual presence of the GC with the AM.
See page 36.

'GAINST ALL DISASTER

GALLANT DEEDS ABOVE & BEYOND THE CALL OF DUTY

★

Allan Stanistreet

PICTON PUBLISHING CHIPPENHAM

1986

Copyright 1986 Allan Stanistreet
First published by Picton Publishing (Chippenham) Ltd 1986
in association with
the Victoria Cross and George Cross Association

ISBN 0 948251 16 6

All rights reserved.
No part of this publication may be reproduced, stored
in a retrieval system, or transmitted, in any form or by any means, electronic,
mechanical, photocopying, recording or otherwise, without the prior
permission of the copyright owner.

Photoset in AM International Plantin
Text paper supplied by Howard Smith Papers, Bristol
Printed in Great Britain by Picton Print
Citadel Works, Bath Road, Chippenham, Wilts
PP52405

Dedicated,
with gracious permission,
to
HER MAJESTY QUEEN ELIZABETH,
THE QUEEN MOTHER

CONTENTS

INTRODUCTION

Many years ago, in 1963 and 1968 respectively, the late Brigadier Sir John Smyth, Bt, VC, MC, wrote the stories of the Victoria Cross and George Cross and their recipients up to those times. Since then, a number of further awards of both decorations have been made and, in October 1971, 132 men and women exchanged their Albert and Edward Medals to become George Cross holders. Not all were happy with the decision over the exchanges and as the wording of the Royal Warrants which authorised the exchanges was permissive, a number of recipients of both the Albert and Edward Medal took advantage of the situation to retain their original awards, despite being considered thenceforth for all official purposes to be holders of the GC.

When the Albert Medal Association was wound up in 1972, the late Commander David Evans, GC, RN (Retired) was requested to compile a book about the gallant deeds of the Albert Medal holders who had been members of that Association and material was slowly gathered through the good offices of many well-wishers. For a variety of reasons, no real progress was made in having this material published until late in 1985, when the compiler, offering typing assistance, found himself with very little time to get something done in time for the VC and GC Association Reunion in May 1986. In the meantime, it had been decided to include all recipients of the VC and GC subsequent to Brigadier Smyth's two volumes mentioned above.

The title of this book is that originally chosen for the book on Albert Medallists and was chosen because it was a line of the famous hymn by John Bunyan which was sung at the first Reunion Service of Rededication after the admission to the VC and GC Association of all previous holders of the Albert and Edward Medals. This took place at St Martin-in-the-Fields on 21st May 1972 and it was generally agreed that such would prove an appropriate title for this book, whilst also reminding members of a very happy and memorable day in the life of the Association. I do not seek to dissent from that choice.

The reader's forebearance is sought if Brigadier Smyth's high standards have not been maintained. I am not a professional writer and most of the work has been done in my spare time over a very short period. Nevertheless, I feel very privileged to have been asked to prepare the book; it has been a most moving and humbling experience reading through the vast amount of material involved and I will never fail to be impressed when meeting the unassuming and charming people who wear these hard-won and well-deserved awards.

Some disparity in length will be noted between the accounts of the different recipients, particularly the exchange awards. This is unfortunately inevitable in a work of this nature, some personalities and events being chronicled better than others. Another important factor is the almost universal reticence of nearly all gallantry award winners and those whose details appear in these pages are no exception to this rule.

I have done my best with the material available and the very limited time at my disposal but I hope my modest efforts will serve to highlight permanently the most gallant deeds of our fellow men and women.

Salisbury, 1986   Allan Stanistreet

THE VICTORIA CROSS

Since the late Sir John Smyth published his book *The Story of the Victoria Cross* in 1963, seven further awards have been made up to the end of 1985. Effectively, these awards span a period of sixteen and a half years, from April 1966 to October 1982 (*London Gazette* dates) and this means roughly one every two years or so.

Four of these VCs were to Australians, all for service in Vietnam, and two of them were posthumous. Of the remainder, two were posthumous awards for the Falkland Islands campaign in 1982. Only two of the seven survive at the end of 1985; Captain (Queen's Gurkha Officer) Rambahadur Limbu, VC, MVO and Warrant Officer Keith Payne, VC.

It is unfortunate that, rightly or wrongly, one of the main qualifications for both the Victoria Cross and George Cross appears to be the demise of the recipient whilst performing the act of gallantry or shortly after and as a direct result of it. This always appeared to be the standard required for both classes of the Albert Medal (q.v.) but surely, it might be argued that the whole point of any award for gallantry is that the recipient should be seen actually wearing the decoration and thereby, presumably, providing an example and inspiration for others. It is questionable whether any useful purpose is served by a gallantry decoration when all, or nearly all, of its recipients die in the act of winning it.

AWARDS: 1963–1985

		London Gazette		
Rambahadur Limbu (MVO)	L/Cpl 2/10 GR	21 Apr 66		3
Wheatley, Kevin Arthur	WO2, AATTV	13 Dec 66	(P)	4
Badcoe, Peter John	Maj, AATTV	13 Oct 67	(P)	5
Simpson, Rayene Stewart (DCM)	WO2, AATTV	29 Aug 69		5
Payne, Keith	WO2, AATTV	19 Sep 69		5
Jones, Herbert (OBE)	Lt-Col, Para	11 Oct 82	(P)	6
McKay, Ian John	Sgt, Para	11 Oct 82	(P)	8

(P) indicates a posthumous award.

Above: Sgt Rambahadur Limbu, VC, and Lt-Col George Styles, GC at Bisley, 1973. Inset: Capt (QGO) Rambahadur Limbu, VC, MVO, on his last day of service, 1985.

The first Victoria Cross to be awarded since the end of the Korean War in 1953 was to a young Lance-Corporal in the Second Battalion 10th (Princess Mary's) Gurkha Rifles. Born on 1st November 1939, Rambahadur Limbu was with an advance party of fourteen Gurkhas on 21st November 1965, when they encountered some thirty Indonesians holding a position on the top of a jungle-covered hill in Sarawak.

Rambahadur went forward with two men. Only ten yards from a sentry with a machine-gun they were seen and the sentry opened fire. Rambahadur rushed forward and killed the sentry with a grenade. The Indonesians then opened fire on Rambahadur's small party, seriously wounding his two companions. Under heavy, aimed small-arms fire, the NCO made two journeys into the open to drag his comrades to safety.

3

Rambahadur Limbu served for over twenty-seven years in the army, reaching the rank of Captain (Queen's Gurkha Officer) and saw service in several active service theatres. Just prior to retirement in 1985, he held the appointment of Queen's Gurkha Orderly Officer, a high honour, and received the MVO for his services. He has now returned to Nepal but two of his sons carry on the family tradition and are now serving with the Brigade of Gurkhas.

WO2 Kevin Wheatley, VC, AATTV.

Maj Peter Badcoe, VC, AATTV.

Four Victoria Crosses were awarded during the terrible and costly so-called Vietnam War, an affair which began at the end of the Second World War, prosecuted first by the French, when the country was known as French Indo-China, and latterly the Vietnamese themselves, aided and supported principally by the Americans. The Australians had an Army Training Team in Vietnam (AATTV), assisting the local forces with advice and expertise and all the Australian awards were to members of this team; the first being posthumously to Warrant Officer Class Two Kevin Arthur Wheatley of the Royal Australian Regiment.

Kevin Wheatley was born in Sydney on 13th March 1937 and educated at Maroubra Junction Technical School, Sydney, working as a brick burner and machine operator until his enlistment into the army in June 1956. His first posting was to the 4th Battalion of the Royal Australian Regiment in September of that year and on 27th March 1957, he joined 3 RAR. He was on operational duty with 3 RAR in Malaya between 1957 and 1959.

Mr Wheatley was appointed Lance-Corporal on 19th January 1959, promoted to Corporal on 2nd February 1959 and Sergeant on 1st January 1964. Promotion to Temporary Warrant Officer Class Two followed on 16th March 1965.

Mr Wheatley was awarded the Victoria Cross for a fine example of loyalty and devotion in refusing to leave a wounded colleague on 13th November 1965, despite overwhelming odds and ample opportunity to make good his escape. He was killed defending his comrade.

A keen sportsman, particularly on the football and rugby fields, his memory was perpetuated in 1967 by the inauguration in Australia of a trophy between the Australian Services

4

Rugby Union and the Sydney Rugby Football Union, to be competed for annually. A sports arena was named after him, which included a bronze plaque describing his action.

Married on 20th July 1954, Kevin Wheatley left a widow, Edna, and four children. He is buried at Pine Grove Memorial Park, Blacktown, New South Wales.

In addition to the Victoria Cross, Warrant Officer Wheatley was awarded the American Silver Star and the Vietnamese Military Merit Medal and Cross of Gallantry with Palm, as well as being created a Knight of the National Order of the Republic of Vietnam.

The next VC for Vietnam was awarded, also posthumously, to Major Peter John Badcoe of the Australian Staff Corps in *The London Gazette* of 13th October 1967. He received the cross for valour on three separate occasions – on 23rd February, 7th March and 7th April 1967. The first occasion, on 23rd February, involved the rescue, under heavy fire, of a United States Medical Adviser, while on 7th March, he personally led his company in an attack and 'turned certain defeat into victory'. His final act of bravery, which resulted in his death, was on 7th April, when he again attempted to lead his company against more powerful opposition. His Cross is one of the rarer ones for sustained gallantry over a period of time, rather than one isolated act.

Major Badcoe was born in Adelaide on 11th January 1934 and went to school there. Starting work as a clerk in the South Australian Public Service, he enlisted into the army in 1952, entering the Officer Cadet School at Portsea, Victoria, on 12th July of that year. He was commissioned as a Second Lieutenant on 13th December 1952.

Most of his regimental postings were with the Royal Australian Artillery and he did two staff jobs before joining the AATTV in August 1966. He was promoted Lieutenant on 13th December 1965, Captain on 29th June 1960 (having been temporary from 8th December 1958), temporary Major on 10th August 1965 and provisional Major on 30th June 1966.

After his death, a number of memorials were created in his memory, including the naming of a training block in his honour at the OCS he had attended. He left a widow, Denise, and three daughters. He, too, received the Silver Star (USA), Order of the Republic of Vietnam, three Crosses of Gallantry (Vietnam) and the Armed Forces Honour Medal, 1st Class. He is buried in the Commonwealth War Graves Commission cemetery at Terendak, near Malacca in Malaysia.

The penultimate Victoria Cross for Vietnam was awarded to Warrant Officer Class Two Rayene Stewart Simpson, a 43-year-old regular soldier serving with the AATT Vietnam. This was for valour on two different occasions – 6th and 11th May 1969. Fortunately, Simpson lived to wear his cross, although, sadly, it was not to be for very long.

On 6th May, he rescued a wounded fellow WO and carried out an unsuccessful attack on a strong enemy position. In the second instance, he fought alone against heavy odds to cover the evacuation of numerous casualties (*London Gazette* 26th August 1969). Warrant Officer Simpson also received the Distinguished Conduct Medal, Silver Star (USA) and Bronze Star (USA) for gallantry in Vietnam. He died in Tokyo on 17th October 1978, at the early age of 52.

The last man to win the VC in Vietnam is Keith Payne, who happily, at the time of writing, is still alive. He was born at Ingham, Queensland on 30th August 1933 and educated at Ingham State School. He became apprenticed as a cabinet-maker but left to join the army on 13th August 1951.

Joining 1st Battalion The Royal Australian Regiment, he served in Korea from April 1952 until March 1953. He was promoted Corporal on 20th January 1955, Sergeant on 1st June

WO2 Rayene Simpson, VC, AATTV.   WO2 Keith Payne, VC, AATTV.

1961 and Temporary Warrant Officer Class Two on 4th June 1965. He was married to Florence Catherine Plaw on 5th December 1954 and they have five sons.

Keith Payne joined the AATTV on 24th February 1969 and three months later, became the 96th Australian to win the Victoria Cross (LG 19th September 1969) when, on 24th May 1969, he demonstrated outstanding courage and leadership in saving many lives of soldiers under his command and leading his men to safety under most difficult circumstances after an attack by the enemy in superior strength.

He also received the Vietnamese Cross for Gallantry, United States Meritorious Unit Citation and Vietnamese Unit Citation Cross of Gallantry. Mr Payne retired from the army on 31st March 1975.

No further awards of the Victoria Cross were made for over twelve years, after Keith Payne's. In early 1982, warlike noises were coming out of Argentina regarding sovereignty over the Falkland Islands. This had long been a contentious issue between Argentina and the United Kingdom and when the Argentinians sent an armed party to South Georgia, followed closely by an invasion force to the Falklands to take possession of these islands, a task force was sent from the United Kingdom by sea to liberate the Falklands and South Georgia from the invader.

Among the infantry units dispatched south was the 2nd Battalion The Parachute Regiment under the command of Lieutenant-Colonel Herbert Jones, OBE.

Herbert Jones was born in Putney on 14th May 1940, the son of Herbert and Olwen Jones. The family moved shortly afterwards to Kingswear in Devon and Herbert Jones went to school first at St Peter's School, Seaford, Sussex and then to Eton College, where he was between September 1953 to March 1958. He entered the Royal Military Academy on leaving school and was commissioned into the Devonshire and Dorset Regiment in July

Lt-Col Herbert Jones, VC, OBE, with his family at Buckingham Palace for his investiture with the OBE.

1960 and spent twenty years with them, until, as a Lieutenant-Colonel, he transferred to the Parachute Regiment.

Colonel Jones served in many parts of the world, including Great Britain, Northern Ireland, British Guiana, Kenya, Australia, Malta, Cyprus and Belize.

He was appointed MBE for services in Northern Ireland after a tour from January 1976 to September 1977 and promoted OBE in the New Year's Honours List of 1981 for his part in planning operations for the peace-keeping force in Zimbabwe. He took over command of the Second Battalion The Parachute Regiment in April 1981.

Married with two sons, Colonel Jones' hobbies included go-karting, motor racing, sailing, cross-country running and military history.

Colonel Jones received the Victoria Cross for valour on 28th May 1982, when he personally led his battalion to victory after it had been held up for over an hour by a superior enemy force. Sadly, he was killed in the very moment of victory but his 'devastating display of courage' as it is described in *The London Gazette*, enabled his battalion to consolidate its gains and force the surrender of some 1,200 men.

The Colonel's Victoria Cross and other medals are now on display in the National Army Museum. He was buried in the War Graves cemetery at San Carlos, Falkland Islands.

In addition to the VC and OBE, Colonel Jones held the General Service Medal with clasp for 'Northern Ireland' and the Queen's Silver Jubilee Medal 1977.

The only other VC to be given for valour during the Falkland Islands campaign was awarded to Sergeant Ian John McKay of the 3rd Battalion The Parachute Regiment; this was also a posthumous award and is the last Victoria Cross awarded as at the end of 1985.

Ian McKay was born on 7th May 1953 at Rotherham in Yorkshire. After attending Roughwood Junior School and Rotherham Grammar School he went straight into the army in September 1970.

His army career progressed very favourably and he received normal promotion up to Sergeant by the time of the Falklands campaign. He was a keen sportsman, enjoying football, tennis, golf, squash and badminton. Amongst his military skills, he was a weapon training instructor.

Sergeant McKay won the Victoria Cross for a most gallant display of leadership and initiative on the night of 11th/12th June 1982, when command of his platoon devolved upon him after its Commander was wounded in the leg. His platoon was pinned down by heavy and accurate enemy fire and realising that unless something was done to resolve the situation, his men could be in great danger, he charged the enemy position alone, several of his companions having been killed or wounded. Like Colonel Jones, he was killed in the moment of victory but his action enabled his comrades to extricate themselves from a most dangerous situation. (LG 8th October 1982)

Ian McKay left a widow, Marica, a daughter and a stepson. His body was brought home for burial, together with those of a number of his fellow soldiers from other regiments as well as his own, and he now lies in the beautiful military cemetery at Aldershot. His VC, General Service Medal for Northern Ireland and South Atlantic Medal with Rosette were loaned by his widow for display in the Imperial War Museum.

Sgt Ian McKay, VC, of the Parachute Regiment.

THE GEORGE CROSS

During the period under review, that is, from the award of the George Cross to Police Constable Gledhill on 23rd May 1967 (covered in Sir John Smyth's book on the GC) to the end of 1985 – some eighteen and a half years – thirteen awards of the George Cross have been made. This is an average of less than one per year.

Sadly, nine recipients have died earning their awards and it is most fervently hoped that the George Cross will not become a reward only for the deceased. No George Crosses have been awarded, as at the end of 1985, for nearly seven years.

AWARDS: 1968–1985

		London Gazette		
Harrison, Barbara Jane	Stewardess, BOAC	8 Aug 69	(P)	11
Willetts, Michael	Sgt, Para	22 Jun 71	(P)	11
Styles, Stephen George	Lt-Col, RAOC	11 Jan 72		12
Emanuel, Errol	District Officer	1 Feb 72	(P)	13
Richardson, Gerald Irving	Supt, Lancs Const	13 Nov 72	(P)	14
Walker, Carl	PC, Lancs Const	14 Nov 72		14
Hudson, Murray Ken	Sgt, RNZIR	26 Sep 74	(P)	14
Beaton, James Wallace	Insp, Met Pol	27 Sep 74		14
Kennedy, James	Sy Offr, BREL	15 Aug 75		15
Goad, Roger Philip (BEM)	ATO, Met Pol	1 Oct 76	(P)	16
Clements, John	Schoolmaster	7 Dec 76	(P)	17
Pratt, Michael Kenneth	Const, Aust Pol	4 Jul 78		17
Nairac, Robert Laurence	Capt, Gren Gds	13 Feb 79	(P)	19

This list excludes exchange awards.   (P) indicates a posthumous award.

Our first award of the GC in this book was to Miss Barbara Jane Harrison, a 22-year-old Stewardess with the British Overseas Airways Corporation (now part of British Airways). On 8th April 1968, the number two engine on Boeing 707 G-ARWE caught fire and fell off soon after take-off and the pilot was obliged to make an emergency landing at Heathrow airport. Miss Harrison's duties in such emergencies were at the aft station in the tail of the aircraft and, surrounded by fire and explosions, she was instrumental in saving the lives of a number of passengers before finally being overcome while trying to save an elderly, crippled passenger, whose body was subsequently found close to that of the Stewardess.

Barbara Jane Harrison, GC.

Nearly two years later came the announcement of the award of the George Cross to Sergeant Michael Willetts of 3rd Battalion The Parachute Regiment. Michael Willetts, a married man with two children, was born on 13th August 1943 and had been a Nottinghamshire miner before becoming a soldier. He had been in Belfast for four months and was on duty in the Springfield Road Police Station on the evening of 25th May 1971, when a terrorist left a smoking suitcase-bomb in the reception hall. Sergeant Willetts, having previously served in Aden and the Radfan, must have been under no illusions as to what might happen. Nevertheless, he stationed himself between the bomb and several civilians

The well-known portrait of Sgt Michael Willetts, GC, 3rd Bn The Parachute Regt.

Michael Willetts as a young soldier (left) with two comrades.

Lt-Col George Styles, GC, with Her Majesty the Queen in June 1972.

and police officers who were evacuating the building, and took the full force of the exploding bomb in order to protect the other people present.

He was buried in his home village of Blidworth, Nottinghamshire. In March 1985, his widow, Sandra, was constrained by financial circumstances to sell his GC and campaign medal, the first George Cross of the present reign to be sold. Happily, it was purchased by the National Army Museum and remains on display in this country.

The second George Cross for service in Northern Ireland was awarded to Major (now Lieutenant-Colonel) Stephen George Styles, RAOC, who was, at the material time, Senior Ammunition Technical Officer, Northern Ireland. George Styles was born on 16th March 1928, attending Collyers Grammar School, Horsham, before joining the King's Own Yorkshire Light Infantry. He subsequently transferred to the Royal Army Ordnance Corps. Colonel Styles is married and has three children.

On 20th and 22nd October 1971, the then Major Styles disarmed two bombs of 10–15 lb and over 30 lb respectively, both equipped with anti-handling devices and taking seven and nine hours respectively to render them harmless. His citation concludes: 'Throughout each operation Major Styles displayed a calm resolution in control, a degree of technical skill and personal bravery in circumstances of extreme danger far beyond that of the call of duty. His work was an outstanding inspiration and example, particularly to others engaged in this dangerous type of work.'

Happily, Colonel Styles survived his many ordeals and now lives quietly at home in the United Kingdom, having retired from the army in 1974, and he lists among his hobbies 'staying married'!

The next GC to be gazetted went posthumously to Errol John Emanuel, an Australian born in Sydney on 13th December 1918. Mr Emanuel joined the Papua New Guinea Administration as a Patrol Officer on 24th August 1946, remaining in this post until 1956, when he was appointed Assistant District Commissioner, an appointment he held until 1965. He was appointed Deputy District Commissioner in 1969 and District Commissioner in 1971. He had on a number of occasions while DC acted as an intermediary between hostile factions in Papua New Guinea, leaving his police protection to do so, well knowing he was risking his life. On 19th August 1971, he once again undertook the role of negotiator between hostile groups but was struck down and mortally wounded. His courage over a long period of time in circumstances of extreme danger

Errol John Emanuel, GC.

was in the highest traditions of the service to which he belonged. Mr Emanuel was survived by a widow and three children.

The third and fourth GCs to be awarded in 1972, a year in which more had been gazetted

Supt Gerald Richardson, GC.

Insp Carl Walker, GC.

than for twenty-five years previously, went to Superintendent Gerald Richardson (posthumously) and Police Constable Carl Walker, both of the Lancashire Constabulary, following an armed robbery at a jewellers in Blackpool on 23rd August 1971.

Mr Richardson, a married man, had joined his local police force in Blackpool as a Cadet after leaving Blackpool Grammar School. He spent his National Service in the Royal Military Police. His promotion was rapid and he had become a Superintendent Class II at the age of only 35, having spent six months at Bramshill Police College in 1963. A keen sportsman, he held the Royal Humane Society's Testimonial on Vellum for a sea rescue on 24th May 1957.

One of Superintendent Richardson's colleagues on 23rd August 1971 was Police Constable Carl Walker. His Panda car was rammed at high speed by the raiders' car in their attempt to escape and when he gave chase on foot, he was shot in the groin and seriously wounded. A married man with one son, Mr Walker was born on 31st March 1934 and was a policeman in Lancashire from 18th October 1954 until he was compelled to retire on medical grounds, as an Inspector, on 30th November 1982. This was as a direct result of the injuries he had sustained during the aforementioned incident.

Sergeant Murray Ken Hudson's posthumous George Cross was gazetted on 26th September 1974. A native-born New Zealander, aged 35, Kena (as he was known) Hudson, born in Opotiki, New Zealand, qualified as a mechanic before joining the army in 1961. He served in Borneo and South Vietnam and he was SAS trained. The incident which won him the George Cross occurred on 13th February 1974, whilst he was supervising live grenade practice with 7 Royal New Zealand Infantry Regiment at Masterton. He became aware that the NCO in his grenade throwing bay had accidentally and perhaps unknowingly armed the grenade he was about to throw. The man appeared to become mesmerised and Sergeant Hudson attempted to force the NCO to throw the grenade over the front parapet of the throwing bay by using his own hands and had almost succeeded when the grenade exploded, killing both men.

Sergeant Hudson must have known he had only four seconds from arming to detonation and gave his life to try to save the

Sgt M. K. Hudson, GC.

other NCO. His was the first George Cross to be awarded for gallantry in New Zealand and he left behind a widow, a son and a daughter.

The next award of a George Cross, happily to a survivor, who gained the Cross for gallantry on 20th March 1974 in a well-publicised incident, was to another police officer.

James Wallace Beaton was born at St Fergus, Aberdeenshire and attended Peterhead

14

An interesting memorial to Sgt Hudson showing his campaign medals for Borneo and Vietnam.

James Wallace Beaton, GC.

Academy in that county. In 1962, he joined the police force and it was as an Inspector in the Metropolitan Police (Royal Bodyguard) that he won his George Cross.

On the evening of 20th March 1974, Her Royal Highness the Princess Anne and her husband, Captain Mark Phillips were returning to Buckingham Palace after an official engagement, when an attempt was made to kidnap Princess Anne. The man fired two handguns at point-blank range, hitting Mr Beaton and three other persons who had come to assist when they heard the commotion. The attempt was thwarted and all concerned behaved with great courage when faced with an unbalanced gunman, including the Princess and her husband; several other persons, including Princess Anne and Captain Phillips, were subsequently decorated for their part in this incident. Chief Superintendent Beaton, as he now is, is a married man with two daughters. His hobbies are reading, gardening and keeping fit.

The following three awards of the George Cross were, sadly, to be posthumous; the first of these was James Stirratt Topping Kennedy. His award, on 15th August 1975, was for great gallantry on 21st December 1973 at British Rail Engineering Limited, Glasgow, where he worked as a Security Officer.

James Kennedy was born in 1930 at Carmunnock, Glasgow and went to school on the Isle of Arran, where he spent much of his early years, and Shawlands Academy School, Glasgow. He had a number of jobs before his National Service in the RAF in 1949 and at the time of the incident, he was a married man with three young daughters.

Above: a proud moment for Mrs Ellen Kennedy, as she unveils the new nameplate on locomotive 86242 at Glasgow Central Station on 12th November 1981. She is watched by her three daughters and James Kennedy's father. Inset: James Kennedy, GC.

Mr Kennedy most courageously tried to prevent an armed robbery at his place of work but was murdered by the gang, all of whom were later caught and sentenced to lengthy terms of imprisonment.

Glasgow Corporation awarded him their Medal for Bravery and on 12th November 1981, British Rail electric express locomotive 86242 was named in his honour by his widow, Ellen, 'James Kennedy, GC'.

In the same month that James Kennedy's GC was gazetted, Captain Roger Goad, BEM, a bomb disposal officer serving with the Metropolitan Police, lost his life attempting to defuse a terrorist bomb in Kensington Church Street. Roger Goad was born on 6th August 1935 and educated at Saltash Grammar School. He joined the army in 1953 and became an Ammunition Technician in the Royal Army Ordnance Corps, being awarded the British Empire Medal as a Sergeant in 1957 for bomb disposal work in Cyprus.

A married man with two daughters, he left the army in 1974 as a Captain and joined the Metropolitan Police as a civilian Explosives Officer. On 29th August 1975, he was called out to deal with a suspect parcel and on his return from this mission, accepted a call to investigate a suspected bomb in a shop doorway. He was just in the process of defusing this device when

Capt Roger Goad, GC, BEM.   John Clements, GC.

it went off and killed him instantly. Those responsible were later apprehended and recommended for minimum terms of thirty years' imprisonment.

John Clements' posthumous award of the George Cross is probably unique for a post-war civilian award in that it was won in a foreign country, i.e. outside the United Kingdom or Commonwealth. Mr Clements was born on 25th August 1953 at Codicote, Hertfordshire, and became a teacher at Sherrardswood School, Welwyn Garden City, Hertfordshire.

He and a party of five other adults and thirty-seven children were on an eight-day visit to the ski resort of Sappada in Northern Italy, when a fire broke out in their hostel early on the morning of 12th April 1976. Mr Clements displayed outstanding gallantry in rescuing and attempting to rescue a number of children and died in the fire whilst making further attempts at rescue, despite efforts to restrain him.

Michael Kenneth Pratt is the youngest surviving holder of the George Cross, having won it whilst serving as a police officer in Victoria, Australia. Born on 13th November 1954, in East Melbourne and educated at The Christian Brothers Parade College, Preston, he joined the Victoria Police Force as a Cadet after two years at the Preston Institute of Technology. He was appointed Constable in March 1974, serving first at Melbourne Traffic and Patrol Division, then in January 1975, he was transferred to Heidelberg.

Mr Pratt, a married man with a son (born in February 1979) was off duty on the morning of 4th June 1976 and he was driving past the ANZ Bank when he noticed an armed robbery

17

The youngest GC, Michael Pratt, meets the oldest VC, Brigadier Sir John Smyth.

Michael Pratt, GC.

Capt Robert Nairac, GC of the Grenadier
Guards.

in progress. Three masked men were involved and Constable Pratt, with great presence of mind and devotion to duty, endeavoured to delay the men's escape and effect the arrest of one or more of them. He was shot and seriously wounded but survived to give evidence at the men's subsequent trial.

Unfortunately, Mr Pratt's injuries were such that he was obliged to leave the police force on medical grounds on 21st July 1979.

The last recipient of the George Cross, up to the time of writing, was yet another posthumous award for Northern Ireland, this time to Captain Robert Laurence Nairac of the Grenadier Guards. He was born on 31st August 1948 in Mauritius, educated at Ampleforth College and Lincoln College, Oxford. Obtaining his commission in 1972, whilst still at Oxford, Robert Nairac joined the Grenadier Guards for duty in 1973, serving with both 1st and 2nd Battalions. During his brief service, he spent over two years in Northern Ireland. He was unmarried.

It was as a Liaison Officer at Headquarters 3 Infantry Brigade that Captain Nairac won his Cross. Whilst on surveillance duties in South Armagh, he was abducted by at least seven men on the night of 14th/15th May 1977 and brutally tortured in an attempt to extract information from him which would have put other lives and future operations at risk. Despite being much weakened physically and after a number of attempts at escape which were thwarted by superior opposite numbers, he was murdered in cold blood by a terrorist specially summoned for the purpose.

Captain Nairac disclosed nothing of value to his captors and behaved in the highest traditions of his regiment and the service, a fact acknowledged subsequently by his abductors.

Since this time, no further awards of the George Cross have been made, up to the end of 1985. It brings the total of direct awards of the Cross, as opposed to exchange awards, to 152.

THE EXCHANGE AWARDS

THE ALBERT MEDAL: 1866–1971

THE EDWARD MEDAL: 1907–1971

In view of the fact that some 132 awards of both the above medals were rendered obsolete at a stroke, as it were, it has been found necessary to adopt a different style to that preceding in order to deal properly with all the recipients who, in fact, only cover a span of just over forty years.

The Albert Medal for Saving Life at Sea.

The Albert Medal for Saving Life on Land.

Obverse and reverse of AM awarded to
Margaret Vaughan showing actual inscription
of deed – unique to this decoration.

THE ALBERT MEDAL

This beautiful and fascinating award was instituted by Royal Warrant dated 7th March 1866 but only one award was made under it – to Samuel Popplestone (LG 13th March 1866). This warrant allowed for only one type of medal: in Gold, for Saving Life at Sea.

The following year another Royal Warrant, dated 12th April 1867, appeared, creating the Albert Medal in two classes: First Class (in Gold) and Second Class (in Bronze). The First Class would be awarded for 'extreme and heroic daring', whereas the Second Class would be for 'acts not sufficiently distinguished to deserve the Albert Medal of the First Class'.

The standard required to qualify for the Albert Medal of the First Class was, throughout its existence, so high that one's survival to wear it was more unlikely than likely. This is witnessed by the fact that during the eighty-three years of its currency, it was only awarded in Gold seventy times.

As has been said, the original AM was created for Saving Life at Sea. In 1877, the need was felt to extend the scope of the medal to acts of gallantry on land and accordingly, such an extension was made by Royal Warrant dated 30th April 1877. There were three differences in the medal; the inscription, the colour of the ribbons for each class and the design of the obverse of the medal itself.

Until 1904, the ribbon for the Second Class had been ⅝-inch in width, an unorthodox and awkward measurement, especially for service personnel. In that year, by Royal Warrant dated 24th March, the ribbon width for the Second Class was altered to 1⅜ inches.

The next change took place by Royal Warrant dated 28th August 1917, when the nomenclature of both classes was changed to 'Albert Medal in Gold' and 'Albert Medal' respectively. At about the same time, the use of the post-nominal initials 'AM' was approved by the King.

The final Royal Warrant relating to the Albert Medal (and Edward Medal) was dated 15th December 1971, effective 21st October 1971, which revoked all existing Royal Warrants and provided for the optional exchange for the George Cross, although all holders, whether they exchanged or not, would be regarded as recipients of the Cross. To their eternal credit, it has to be said, 15 Albert Medallists elected to retain their original awards, the remaining 49 individuals exchanging them – a total of 64 persons eligible.

It was argued by the protagonists for the exchange that, *inter alia,* hardly anybody then living realised the status of the AM. Indeed, its status had been much reduced by the exchanges, in 1940, of the Empire Gallantry Medal for the George Cross. There were, in fact, a number of instances where both Albert Medals and Empire Gallantry Medals had been given for the same incident; presumably those who received the EGM were deemed to have performed less worthy acts by the standards of the time than those who received the AM. The effect of the 1940 GC Warrant was immediately to reverse this order of things – an invidious state of affairs, to say the least and without wishing any disrespect to any of those decorated.★

★See article 'All Shall Equal Be . . .' by J. M. A. Tamplin in the *Journal of the Orders and Medals Research Society,* Winter 1978, Vol 17, No 4.

It is quite incredible that those responsible for these matters down the years apparently never stopped to review the situation. As a result, the whole system for awarding medals for 'civilian' gallantry, if one may use such a word, got into the most incredible mess. At one stage, there were no fewer than eleven awards available for 'civilian' gallantry and, quite plainly, something had to be done. However, this lamentable state of affairs dragged on for some years after the Albert and Edward Medal exchanges and was not finally resolved until the institution of the Queen's Gallantry Medal in 1974, which finally, at least as far as 'civilian' gallantry was concerned, divorced the degree of bravery displayed from the imagined social class.

A few general points relating to the Albert Medal may be of interest to readers at this stage. Firstly, it is an extremely rare medal, in either Gold or Bronze and neither class was lightly bestowed. It is far rarer than the Victoria Cross, the numbers awarded being:

$$
\begin{array}{llll}
\text{Gold} & - & \text{Sea} & - & 25 \\
& & \text{Land} & - & 45
\end{array} = 70
$$
$$
\begin{array}{llll}
\text{Bronze} & - & \text{Sea} & - & 215 \\
& & \text{Land} & - & 285
\end{array} = 500
$$
$$= 570$$

Only five Gold medals were awarded between 1919 and 1949, when Gold awards ceased; one every six years. Three were sea awards and two land, of which both the latter were posthumous. One was to Sick Berth Attendant Arturo Fanconi, RN, (LG 15th May 1945) and was the last Gold AM ever awarded. The last Gold AM awarded to a living recipient was to Sick Berth Attendant G. W. Beeching, RN, (LG 20th April 1943). The last surviving recipient of the Albert Medal in Gold was Major Thomas Barnard Hankey, MC, AM, of the KRRC, who won his medal in the First World War and died in a nursing home in Swindon in 1969. There were therefore no Albert Medals in Gold exchanged for the George Cross.

No bars were ever awarded to either class of Albert Medal and no provision was ever made for them in any of the Royal Warrants.

The most Albert Medals awarded for one incident was in *The London Gazette* of 7th August 1877, when no less than four Gold and *twenty-two* Bronze medals were awarded for a mine disaster in South Wales. There were other multiple awards but this number was never exceeded during the life of the AM and has only been equalled by multiple awards of the Edward Medal (q.v.) and Sea Gallantry Medal.

In 1949, His Majesty King George VI decided that no further awards of the Albert Medal in Gold would be made and those of the Second Class or Bronze Medal would be posthumous only. This was allegedly because of the plethora of gallantry awards then available for rewarding acts not performed in the presence of an enemy (*vide supra*). The last award made to a living recipient, therefore, was to Margaret Vaughan in *The London Gazette* of 1st January 1949.

The very last (posthumous) Albert Medal award was to Kenneth Owen McIntyre in *The London Gazette* of 11th August 1970.

At the time of writing, there are still three people (all men) wearing their original award of the Albert Medal (see text). Of the 64 persons originally eligible to exchange their medals, 29 were Royal Navy, its Reserves, RNAS or RM, 12 were Army, including Commonwealth, 5 were RFC or RAF and 18 were civilians, including Merchant Navy.

Sixteen ladies were awarded the AM, all in Bronze and two being posthumous awards. Five survived to exchange it for the GC, of whom two are now still living.

Thomas William McCORMACK, GC (formerly AM)

Thomas William McCormack was born on 23rd February 1886. Nothing is known of his early life on Tyneside but he was to become a dockyard labourer at Jarrow and it was in this capacity that he was to win the Albert Medal for Gallantry on Saving Life on land.

For this act Mr McCormack also received the Bronze Medal of the Carnegie Hero Fund Trust, believed to be the first of these medals ever awarded.

At the time of conversion of his Albert Medal for the George Cross, Mr McCormack's act of gallantry was then the earliest known to have a surviving Albert or Edward Medallist and the exchange was made over sixty-three years after the actual event.

Thomas McCormack was married with a son and three daughters. He was a member of the Albert Medal Association and died, aged 87, at his home in Jarrow, County Durham.

Thomas McCormack, GC.

The citation for his Albert Medal reads as follows:

'On 27th November 1908, workmen were engaged in painting the inside of an iron tank in the stokehold of a steamer lying in dry dock at Jarrow. Owing to the fact that very strong fumes were given off by the anti-corrosive paint or solution used, the men were working in relays, each squad of three men being relieved after ten or fifteen minutes had elapsed. A workman named Graham was overcome by the fumes, and the charge-man, Archibald Wilson, sacrificed his life in endeavouring to save Graham. Thomas McCormack, who had already been affected by the fumes while at work in the tank, went to Wilson's assistance, but was himself rendered insensible, and was rescued by James Kennedy Chapman, Works Manager at the Dock, who, having pulled McCormack out, re-entered the tank and endeavoured to save Graham, but was himself overcome by fumes. The rescue of Chapman and Graham was eventually effected from the top of the tank.' (LG 23rd July 1909)

James Kennedy Chapman and Archibald Wilson (posthumously) were both awarded the Albert Medal for their gallantry.

Hilda Elizabeth WOLSEY, GC (formerly AM)

Hilda Wolsey was born on 26th June 1887. She qualified as a nurse and was working at Hanwell Asylum (now St Bernard's Hospital), Southall, Middlesex, when she won the Albert Medal for a gallant rescue.

Hilda Wolsey, GC.

'On the 11th of June 1910, a female patient at the Hanwell Asylum, while exercising in one of the airing courts, climbed over the wire covering of one of the fire-escape staircases, and, reaching the roof of the laundry ward, ran along the narrow guttering at the edge of the roof. Nurse Wolsey followed her over the wire covering of the escape, and along the narrow guttering, twenty-five feet above the ground, making her way by leaning with one hand against the sloping roof, and, reaching the patient, held her, at great personal risk, until ropes and ladders were procured and she was lowered to safety.' (LG 28th March and 26th May 1911)

She was the second senior living Albert Medal recipient (and the senior of the ladies to do so) after Mr McCormack (q.v.) to exchange her medal for the George Cross, which she did in 1972. She subsequently presented her medal to the St Bernard's Hospital, where it is now on display.

Hilda Wolsey was a very independent lady and would not go to Buckingham Palace for investiture with the GC 'for fear of being a nuisance and embarrassing the Queen'! She similarly declined any special ceremony for the presentation of her AM to the hospital.

She died at Ealing, London, on 11th March 1974, aged 86.

Michael Sullivan KEOGH, GC, OBE (formerly AM)

Michael Sullivan Keogh was born in County Cork, Ireland, on 15th May 1889. Nothing is known of his early life but he joined the Royal Naval Air Service on 23rd April 1910 as a Petty Officer, carpenter's crew, for twelve years' service. He was subsequently promoted to Chief Petty Officer, though the date is not known. Rated as a Leading Mechanic on 1st July 1914, he was promoted temporary Warrant Officer Class Two for carpenter's duties on 7th May 1917.

Michael Keogh had qualified as a pilot in 1913 and by 1915, he was serving in the Mediterranean, where he won the Albert Medal.

'On the 19th of August 1915, an aeroplane, piloted by the late Captain C. H. Collett, DSO, RMA, was ascending from the Island of Imbros Aerodrome, and had reached a height of 150 feet when the engine stopped. The machine was upset by the powerful air currents from the cliffs, and fell vertically to the ground, while the petrol carried burst into flames which immediately enveloped the aeroplane and pilot.

Chief Petty Officer Keogh, of HMS *Ark Royal*, at once attempted to save Captain Collett by dashing into the midst of the wreckage, which was a mass of flames. He had succeeded in dragging the fatally injured officer nearly clear of the flames when he was himself overcome by the burns which he had received from the blazing petrol.' (LG 14th January and 19th May 1916)

Between 1917 and 1918, WO Keogh served at Crystal Palace and Tregantle on carpenter's duties. However, on 1st April 1918, he was commissioned into the Royal Air Force as a Second Lieutenant, Technical

Group Captain M. S. Keogh, GC,
OBE as a PO, RN.

Officer. After commissioning, he went to RAF Halton, where he appears to have remained until 1924, when he went to Henlow for a twelve-month course, then to Karachi.

Returning to Uxbridge in 1938, by which time he was a Flight Lieutenant, he was supernumerary from March to October 1930, when he went back to Henlow. Various postings followed in UK and he then spent three years in Singapore, from 1936 to 1939. He had been promoted Squadron Leader in 1937.

Placed on the Retired List in May 1939, he was appointed to a Short Service Commission in the Royal New Zealand Air Force in June 1939, where he remained until 1947, retiring as a Group Captain with the OBE. He returned to the UK, living in Kent after retirement, where he died, aged 94, on 22nd July 1983.

Group Captain Keogh's awards included the 1914 Star with bar, British War, Victory and Queen's Silver Jubilee Medals. His Albert Medal is now on display at the Royal Air Force Museum, Hendon.

Harrie Stephen HARWOOD, GC (formerly AM)

Harrie Stephen Harwood was born on 10th July 1884 at Whitwell, Yorkshire and was educated at Worcester Grammar School. His early years after leaving school were spent in the Audit Department of the North Staffordshire Railway Company.

During the First World War, he served with the Royal Flying Corps, first as a Despatch Rider and then, in the autumn of 1916, he became an Observer. Returning to England, he was commissioned on 6th March 1917. He learnt to fly at Sledgeford.

In 1916, First Class Air Mechanic Harwood was stationed at St Omer in France and, together with three others, was awarded the Albert Medal for gallantry at a bomb store. The story runs as follows:

'On the 3rd January, 1916, at about 3pm, a fire broke out inside a large bomb store belonging to the Royal Flying Corps, which contained nearly 2,000 high explosive bombs, some of which had very large charges, and a number of incendiary bombs, which were burning freely. Major Newall at once took all necessary precautions, and then, assisted by Air Mechanic Simms, poured water into the shed through a hole made by the flames. He sent for the key of the store, and with Corporal Hearne, Harwood and Simms entered the building and succeeded in putting out the flames. The wooden cases containing the bombs were burnt, and some of them were charred to a cinder. (LG 19th May 1916)

Harrie Harwood, GC.

Major Cyril Norton Newall, 2nd Gurkha Rifles (attached RFC), who died on 30th November 1963 as Marshal of the Royal Air Force Lord Newall, GCB, OM, GCMG, CBE, AM, was awarded the Albert Medal in Gold; and Corporal Henry Hearne, RFC and 2nd Class Air Mechanic Alfred Edward Simms, RFC, (died 1969) the Albert Medal.

Mr Harwood returned to the North Staffordshire Railway after the war, the company being absorbed, in 1923, into the London Midland and Scottish Railway. He was married to Gladys (née Godwin) and they had a son and a daughter.

In 1940, Harrie Harwood joined the Royal Air Force as a Recruiting Officer, being stationed first at Ipswich and later in Norwich. Towards the end of the war, he became an RTO, serving in Manchester, Preston and Liverpool. He was demobilised in early 1947 in the rank of Flight Lieutenant.

In addition to his Albert Medal, he held the 1914–15 Star, British War Medal, Victory Medal, Defence Medal, War Medal. His Albert Medal is now on display in Etruscan Lodge No 546, Masonic Hall, Shelton.

He died, after a long illness, at Didcot, Oxfordshire, on 13th November 1975, aged 91.

Albert FORD, GC (formerly AM)

Albert Ford was born at Stoke-on-Trent, Staffordshire, in March 1894.

He enlisted in the Royal Welch Fusiliers in 1915 and was demobilised as a Company Sergeant-Major in 1919. He was married with a son and two daughters: his wife died in November 1968, after fifty-four years of marriage.

Mr Ford was awarded the Albert Medal for gallantry on 30th May 1916.

'On 30th May 1916, while a class of men was under instruction in bombing at Gorre in

France, a member of the class hit with his bomb the traverse in front of him, so that the smoking bomb fell into the trench. The man immediately ran away, knocking down Sergeant Ford, R. Welch Fusiliers, who was acting as instructor. Ford at once recovered his feet, pushed past the man, and managed to pick up the bomb and throw it clear; it exploded immediately it left his hand.' (LG 21st August 1917)

Albert Ford, GC, and family, outside Buckingham Palace.

Mr Ford suffered severe wounds two weeks after this incident. He was invested with the George Cross on 18th July 1972 and his Albert Medal is now on display in the City Museum, Hanley, Stoke-on-Trent. He also held the 1914–15 Star, British War and Victory Medals. Albert Ford died at Stoke-on-Trent in July 1976, aged 82.

George Faucett Pitts ABBOTT, GC (formerly AM)
Richard John KNOWLTON, GC (formerly AM)

'On the 14th September 1917, a seaplane collided with a Poulsen mast and remained wedged in it, the pilot (Acting Flight Commander E. A. de Ville) being rendered unconscious and thrown out of his seat on to one of the wings.

The three men above mentioned* at once climbed up the mast for 100 feet, when Rath, making use of the boatswain's chair, which moves on the inside of the mast, was hoisted up by men at the foot of the mast to the place, over 300 feet from the ground, where the seaplane was fixed. He then climbed out on the plane, and held the pilot until the arrival of Knoulton [sic] and Abbott, who passed the masthead gantline out to him.

Having secured the pilot with the gantline Rath, with the assistance of Knoulton [sic] and Abbott, lifted him from the plane to the inside of the mast and lowered him to the ground.

R. J. Knowlton, GC.

29

AB G. F. P. Abbott, AM at the time of his award.

Geoffrey Abbott shows his Albert Medal.

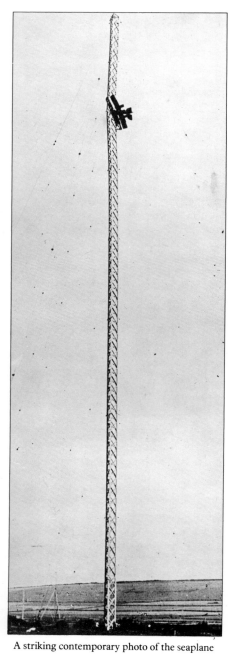

A striking contemporary photo of the seaplane stuck in the Poulsen mast.

The three men were very well aware of the damaged and insecure condition of the mast, which was bent to an angle where the seaplane had become wedged. One of the three supports of the mast was fractured, and, so far as the men knew, the mast or seaplane might at any time have collapsed.' (LG 14th December 1917)

*Nicholas Rath, Ordinary Seaman, RNR, received the Albert Medal in Gold for this incident and the two men mentioned above received the Albert Medal.

George Faucett Pitts Abbott was born in Nelson, Lancashire, on 18th September 1898 and educated at Whitefield School in the town. In civilian life, he was a cotton operative until 1916, when, on 21st August, he joined the Royal Naval Reserve as a Deckhand, continuing his service until 22nd July 1919.

In 1921, Mr Abbott married Alice Emily Harris and they had one daughter. He declined to exchange his Albert Medal in 1971 and held in addition to the AM, the British War Medal, Victory Medal and Queen's Silver Jubilee Medal 1977. His hobbies included walking, gardening, snooker and horse racing. He died of emphysema on 10th June 1977.

Richard John Knowlton was born on 11th May 1899 and attended Bursledon Village School in Hampshire. His early life is something of a mystery but he was in the Royal Navy by 1917, serving as an Ordinary Seaman, when he won his Albert Medal.

Mr Knowlton left the Royal Navy as an AB (Torpedoman) at the end of the war in 1919 and joined the Southampton Fire Brigade as a fireman/driver. He remained in that post until 1929 when he went to Salisbury as a Station Officer. He left Salisbury in 1941 to become a Section Leader in the National Fire Service and Sub Officer in Wiltshire Fire Brigade, until his retirement in 1954.

In 1923, he married Florence Humby and they had two sons and two daughters.

Besides the Albert Medal, which he, too, declined to exchange, Mr Knowlton had the British War Medal, Victory Medal and Queen's Silver Jubilee Medal 1977. The family has inherited a piece of the propellor from the crashed plane.

Richard Knowlton (the correct spelling of his surname – it has been incorrectly spelt on numerous occasions over the years, including in the *London Gazette* citation and on his AM) died at Wolverhampton on 24th August 1981, aged 82.

Doreen ASHBURNHAM, GC (formerly AM)

Doreen Ashburnham was born, an only child, on 13th May 1905 at Ashburnham Hall in Sussex and when she was nine, her parents took her, for the sake of her health, to live on Vancouver Island in Canada. Doreen was a grand-niece on Lieutenant-Colonel Sir Joseph and Lady Fayrer of Edinburgh.

It was whilst walking in woods near her home with her younger cousin that Doreen performed the deed which won for her the Albert Medal. *The London Gazette* puts things very succinctly:

'On the 23rd of September 1916, two children, Doreen, aged 11 and Anthony, aged 8, left their homes at Cowichan Lake, Vancouver Island, for the purpose of catching their ponies and, when half a mile from home, they were attacked by a large cougar. They

Anthony Farrer and Doreen Ashburnham just after being presented with the medals by the Duke of Devonshire.

The inn sign formerly at Street in Somerset.

were almost upon the animal before they saw it crouching in a path at a corner. The little girl was first attacked; the cougar sprang upon her, and she was knocked down with her face to the ground, the animal being on her back. The boy at once attacked the cougar with his fists and riding bridle, and drove the animal off the girl; it then attacked him, and his companion, getting to her feet, came to his rescue, fighting with her clenched hands and bridle, and even putting her arm into the cougar's mouth, to try to prevent it from biting Anthony. She succeeded in getting it off the boy and it stood on its hind quarters and fought with her but evidently it was disturbed by some sound, for presently it slunk away and ran under a log, where it was afterwards killed. The children, though both badly injured, were able to make their way home.' (LG 21st December 1917)

Anthony Farrer also received the Albert Medal, he being the youngest person ever to receive a British gallantry decoration while Doreen was the youngest-ever female recipient. They were presented with their medals by His Grace the Duke of Devonshire, on behalf of His Majesty. Anthony Farrer was particularly badly injured by the cougar and spent a long period in hospital. Sadly, he was killed in 1930, aged 21, whilst on army manoeuvres in Canada.

Doreen Ashburnham continued to live at Lake Cowichan until 1925, where she attended St Margaret's School, Victoria. In that year, she returned to England as a débutante to be presented to His Majesty King George V. Returning to live in California, where she and her family had previously spent winters, she became a member of the first women's polo team in the United States. Subsequently, she lived for a time in Italy, where she raised show horses and rode in international competitions both in England and mainland Europe. In 1935, she trained as a pilot and during the Second World War ferried military aircraft from the United States to Europe.

Miss Ashburnham married a college languages professor called Ruffner in 1942 and they had a daughter after the end of the war. They live in San Pedro, California and Mrs Ashburnham-Ruffner is now a citizen of the United States.

It was some time after the Albert Medal exchange was announced that Mrs Ashburnham-Ruffner heard about the matter and she received her GC in May 1974, being awarded the Queen's Silver Jubilee Medal in 1977. She presented her Albert Medal for display in the Canadian War Museum in Ottawa in 1974.

Mrs Doreen Ashburnham-Ruffner, GC, pictured in October 1983.

On 21st November 1975, a most unusual tribute was paid in England to the two brave children, when the Courage Brewery named one of their public houses 'The Albert Inn'. The public house is at Street, in Somerset, and the sign was unveiled by Rear-Admiral R. W. Armytage, GC, CBE (q.v.). The sign was unfortunately removed during renovations in July 1985 and has not, it appears, been reinstated.

William Ernest RHOADES, GC (formerly AM)

William Ernest Rhoades was born on 6th February 1888 and attended Holy Trinity School at Eastbourne. In 1902, he became a mechanic with the Eastbourne Motor Company, until 1909, when he went into service as a chauffeur/mechanic, a position he held until his retirement in 1951.

He served in the Royal Flying Corps between October 1914 and April 1919 and in the Honours List of 1st January 1919, was awarded the Meritorious Service Medal. He finished his war service as a Warrant Officer Class One (Technical Sergeant-Major).

His Albert Medal was won in France on 14th October 1916, in the following circumstances:

'At an aerodrome in France, on the 14th October, 1916, a bomb accidentally exploded in the mouth of a dug-out forming a bomb store, which contained a large number of bombs packed in wooden cases and a quantity of rockets. Two men were killed by the explosion, and another man, who was severely injured, was thrown down into the store. Dense volumes of smoke issued from the dug-out, and there was a great risk of a further explosion. Lieutenant (then Second Lieutenant) Smith, on hearing a call for help, immediately entered the dug-out, followed by Sergeant Rhoades, and succeeded in rescuing the wounded man, who would otherwise have been suffocated.' (LG 1st January 1918)

William Rhoades, AM.

W. E. Rhoades, GC, with his wife and daughter.

Lieutenant Frederick Stuart Smith, RFC, also received the Albert Medal for this incident and both he and Rhoades suffered from lung trouble for many years as a result of inhaling the acrid smoke in 1916.

Mr Rhoades was married and he and his wife, Marion, had one daughter. During the Second World War, he served as a Lieutenant in the Home Guard. He was a founder member of the Albert Medal Association but did not exchange his AM, in addition to which he also held the 1914 Star, British War Medal, Victory Medal and Meritorious Service Medal.

His hobbies were reading and gardening and he died at Eastbourne on 4th March 1972, aged 84.

Richard Leslie BROWN, GC (formerly AM)

Richard Leslie Brown was born on 28th May 1898 in Huddersfield, Yorkshire and educated at Tideswell School, Derby. During the First World War, he was commissioned into the Royal Lancaster Regiment and it was as a subaltern in France that he won his Albert Medal. His citation reads:

'In France, on 27th March, 1917, Lieutenant Brown was instructing a class in firing rifle grenades. Owing to a defective cartridge one of the grenades was lifted only about two inches, and then fell back into the cup. The safety catch had been released and the grenade was fusing. Lieutenant Brown at once ordered the men to clear and, running forward, picked up the rifle, seized it between his legs, grasped the grenade in his hands and endeavoured to throw it away. While he was doing so it exploded, blowing off his right hand and inflicting other wounds. Had not Lieutenant Brown seized the grenade in his hand, thus sheltering the men, there can be little doubt that several of them would have been killed or severely injured.' (LG 4th January 1918)

After demobilisation, Mr Brown joined the firm of Hopkinsons Limited of Huddersfield as an engineer. He became a director of the company in 1928, being appointed deputy managing director in 1929 and managing director in 1933. He became chairman of the board in 1942 and retired in 1972. He was appointed the first Honorary President of Hopkinsons Holdings Limited, an associated company of Hopkinsons Limited, in 1973.

Richard Brown, GC.

Mr Brown went to live at Annan in Dumfries-shire with his wife, and died there on 25th September 1982. They had no children. His hobbies were shooting and fishing and he was awarded the Queen's Silver Jubilee Medal in 1977. His Albert Medal is now on display in the regimental museum of the King's Own Border Regiment.

Albert James HUTCHISON, GC (formerly AM)

Albert James Hutchison was born in 1892. Nothing is known of his early life but he served in the Highland Light Infantry during the First World War and it was as a Sergeant in that regiment that he won the Albert Medal in 1917.

'At the Curragh Camp, Ireland, on the 2nd April 1917, during bombing practice, a live grenade hit the parapet of the trench and fell back at the feet of the man who had thrown it. The man was too terrified to move, and obstructed the efforts of Sergeant Hutchison to pick up the bomb. After the fuse had been burning for three seconds, Sergeant Hutchison managed to push the man away, pick up the bomb, and throw it over the parapet, where it immediately exploded. But for the Sergeant's coolness and gallantry the man would undoubtedly have been killed or severely injured.' (LG 4th January 1918)

After the war, he returned to the United Kingdom and worked for the Yorkshire Electricity Board for thirty years.

Mr Hutchison donated his Albert Medal to the Royal Highland Fusiliers Museum in Glasgow and died on 9th June 1975, at Kilcreggan, Dumbartonshire.

Oliver Campbell BRYSON, GC, MC, DFC, (formerly AM)

Oliver Campbell Bryson was born on 18th August 1896, the second son of George Bryson, a hardware merchant of Birmingham, and his wife, Edith, who was the daughter of a well-known silversmith in Birmingham, George Unite. They lived at The Oaks, Lickey, a few miles from Birmingham and later moved into a larger home at Burnt Green. When Oliver was thirteen, his mother died, at an early age, of tuberculosis.

Oliver Bryson attended Lickey Hills Preparatory School and later Uppingham. He passed into Trinity College, Cambridge but the First World War intervened. He joined the Dorset Yeomanry at the outbreak of war and served in the Egyptian theatre, being wounded in the cavalry charge at Oggagia in 1916. He won the MC in France in 1918 (LG 4th February 1918).

By 1917, Lieutenant Bryson had transferred to the Royal Flying Corps and he won his Albert Medal whilst serving with them in 1917.

Flt Lt O. C. Bryson, MC, DFC, AM, RAF.

'On the 15th March 1917, Captain (then Lieutenant) Bryson, with Second Lieutenant Hillebrandt as passenger, was piloting an aeroplane at Wye Aerodrome when, owing to a sideslip, the machine crashed to the ground and burst into flames. On disentangling himself from the burning wreckage Captain Bryson at once went back into the flames, dragged Lieutenant Hillebrandt from the machine, and, notwithstanding his own injuries, which were undoubtedly aggravated by his gallant efforts to rescue his brother officer from the fire, endeavoured to extinguish the fire on Lieutenant Hillebrandt's clothing.

Lieutenant Hillebrandt succumbed to his injuries a few days later.' (LG 11th January 1918)

Oliver Bryson was married for the first time to Cecile Allen, an American girl whom he met in Paris. They were married in St George's, Hanover Square, London on 27th July 1927, the bride being only eighteen years of age. The Brysons had one daughter, Daphne, who was born in June 1930, when her father was serving in the RAF at Quetta. There was subsequently a divorce, although Oliver and his former wife remained on good terms until her sudden death in Bermuda in 1976. He married again after the Second World War but nothing is known of the union.

Oliver Bryson served on the North West Frontier of India during the 1930s and was awarded a bar (LG 26th June 1931) to the DFC which he had won in 1919 (LG 18th

November 1919). He remained in the RAF until retirement in 1946 with the rank of Group Captain. His hobbies were horse racing, bee keeping and dog breeding.

Although his Albert Medal was believed lost at the time of the exchange and he was invested with the George Cross, the medal appears to have remained firmly fixed to the mounting bar with his other awards, presenting the unusual spectacle at auction in November 1985 of both awards for the same act of gallantry (see frontispiece). His other medals, apart from those already mentioned, were: 1914–15 Star, British War Medal, Victory Medal, India General Service Medal (clasp 'Mohmand 1931'), Defence Medal, War Medal, Coronation Medal 1937.

Group Captain Oliver Campbell Bryson, GC, MC, DFC and Bar, died in Guildford on 27th March 1977.

Paul Douglas ROBERTSON, GC, CBE, (formerly AM)

Paul Douglas Robertson was born in Willesden, Middlesex, on 30th April 1891 and educated in London, Jamaica and Australia. He was the son of Captain William Foy Robertson, a Master Mariner of Scottish descent.

Paul Robertson joined the Royal Navy at the age of 19 and on 9th February 1916, as a Flight Lieutenant, RN, was awarded his aviator's certificate. By early 1918, he was an Acting Flight Commander, Royal Naval Air Service, in command of Hornsea Mere Sub-Station. It was in this appointment that he won the Albert Medal, suffering the loss of one eye in so doing. The medal was presented to him by King George V at Buckingham Palace on 31st October 1918.

Lt P. D. Robertson, AM, RNAS.

Gp Capt P. D. Robertson, AM, 1941.

37

'On the 28th February 1918, a seaplane got out of control and spun to the ground. Acting Flight Commander Robertson, the observer, jumped from the machine just before it reached the ground and landed safely, as the ground was marshy. The pilot, Flight Lieutenant H. C. Lemon, was imprisoned in the seaplane, which, on striking the ground, immediately burst into flames, and notwithstanding that the vicinity of the seaplane was quickly a furnace of blazing petrol, and that heavy bombs, a number of rounds of ammunition, and the reserve petrol tank were all likely to explode, Acting Flight Commander Robertson returned and endeavoured to extricate the pilot, and only desisted when he had been so severely burned in the face, hands and leg that his recovery was for some time in doubt.

He displayed the greatest gallantry, self-sacrifice and disregard of danger in his efforts to extricate the pilot.' (LG 18th January 1918)

Paul Robertson married Edna Lilian Maxwell Dalton, daughter of the Governor of Suva Gaol, Fiji, on 23rd February 1915 at Cransley Parish Church, Northamptonshire. They had three children, two daughters and a son, the latter unfortunately accidentally killed while still at school, aged 9, in 1934. Robertson's first wife died after a fall in December 1963 and he married again in 1966.

Group Captain Robertson spent his entire career in the Royal Air Force, specialising in navigation training, until his retirement in December 1945. He commanded the School of Air Navigation in Canada, later in Squire's Gate, near Blackpool and was appointed CBE on 1st January 1944, which he received from King George VI at Buckingham Palace in March 1944. Other medals he received included the British War Medal, Mercantile Marine War Medal, Victory Medal, Defence Medal, War Medal (Mentioned in Despatches, 1943) and Coronation Medal 1937. His hobbies were sailing, fishing, reading, painting, carpentry and model-making. Despite the loss of an eye, he was a competent pilot and painted beautifully.

His GC was exchanged by post in 1972, since he was not well enough to travel to London for investiture and he died in Auckland, New Zealand, where he had spent the last few years of his life, on 4th August 1975, aged 84.

Alfred William NEWMAN, GC (formerly AM)

Alfred William Newman was born on 11th April 1888 at Empingham in Rutland. He attended Empingham School and Andrew Judd Commercial School, Tonbridge, Kent. Commander Newman joined the Royal Navy in 1903 as a boy, earning 6d (2½p) per week and served in both world wars, although from 1923 until 1939 he had his own poultry farming business. He married his wife, Alice May, in 1919 and they had a son and a daughter. Mrs Newman died in December 1973.

In 1939, Alfred Newman rejoined the Navy and was found to be one of the few officers qualified in the construction of anti-torpedo nets for harbour defence. He was appointed to supervise net construction for the whole of the United Kingdom. After this, he was appointed Naval Officer of Harbour Defences for Gambia and, in 1943, was drafted to Aden to take charge, under the Commodore there, of harbour defences from Suez to Bangkok. He retired again in April 1948, aged 60, with the rank of Commander.

Commander Newman won his Albert Medal in 1917 as Mate on board HMS *Tetrarch* and

Sub Lt A. W. Newman, AM, RN, about 1918.

Cdr A. W. Newman, GC, July 1972.

was decorated by His Majesty King George V on board HMS *Curacoa* in Harwich Harbour in February 1918.

> 'On the 10th October, 1917, an alarm of fire was given in the after magazine of one of HM ships. Mr Alfred William Newman, Acting Mate, RN, who was on the upper deck, proceeded to the magazine as soon as he heard the alarm, and, seeing smoke issuing from a box of cordite, opened the lid and passed the cartridges on to the upper deck, where they were thrown overboard. One cartridge in the middle of the box was very hot, and smoke was issuing from the end. It is considered that, by his prompt and gallant action, Mr Newman saved the magazine from blowing up and the loss of many lives.' (LG 5th March 1918)

Commander Newman held the 1914–15 Star, British War Medal, and Victory Medal, besides his AM, which is now in the National Maritime Museum, with his George Cross. He also held the Marine Society's Reward of Merit for 1908 but did not claim his Second World War campaign medals.

He lived in Surrey in the closing years of his life, and enjoyed gardening, wood-carving and sewing sail-cloth shopping bags until he was 93. He died at East Grinstead on 1st September 1984, aged 96.

Victor Albert WATSON, GC (formerly AM)

Victor Albert Watson was born in 1897; nothing is known of his early life and education. He served in the Royal Navy during the First World War and won the Albert Medal in 1918.

'On the occasion of an accident to one of His Majesty's Airships, which resulted in a fire breaking out on board her, Flight Lieutenant Watson, who was the senior Officer on the spot, immediately rushed up to the car of the airship under the impression that one of the crew was still in it, although he was well aware that there were heavy bombs attached to the airship which it was impossible to remove owing to the nearness of the fire, and which were almost certain to explode at any moment on account of the heat. Having satisfied himself that there was in fact no one in the car, he turned away to render assistance elsewhere, and at that moment one of the bombs exploded, a portion of it shattering Lieutenant Watson's right arm at the elbow. The arm had to be amputated almost immediately.' (LG 8th March 1918)

V. A. Watson, GC.

Harold Victor Robinson and Eric Edward Steere received the Albert Medal in Gold for their part in this incident.

Mr Watson was invested with the AM in 1918 and elected to retain his original award in 1971. He died in London on 3rd October 1974, aged 77, and was cremated at Golders Green Crematorium.

Thomas Neil DAVIS, GC (formerly AM)

Thomas Neil Davis was born on 18th May 1895. He was brought up in an orphanage at Weston, near Crewe, in Cheshire. Little is known of his early life but by 1915 he was serving in the Royal Naval Reserve No J.18334 (Dev.). In 1917, he was a Leading Seaman on board HMS *Highflier*, moored in Halifax Harbour, Nova Scotia, when the event occurred which resulted in the award of six Albert Medals, one in gold. Three of these awards, including the gold one, were posthumous.

'On the 6th December 1917, the French steamer *Mont Blanc*, with a cargo of high explosives, and the Nor-

Lt-Cdr T. N. Davis, GC.

40

wegian steamer *Imo*, were in collision on Halifax Harbour. Fire broke out on the *Mont Blanc* immediately after the collision, and the flames very quickly rose to a height of 100 feet. The crew abandoned their ship and pulled to the shore. A few minutes later a tremendous explosion took place, and the tug *Musquash* was seen to be on fire forward. The fire was increasing and there appeared to be a great danger of her getting adrift, and being carried down on to another vessel. As the *Musquash* had a gun and ammunition on board there was a danger of a further explosion and consequent loss of life.

The captain of HMS *Highflier* hailed a private tug and asked her to take the *Musquash* in tow, but as they were unwilling to board the *Musquash* to get her in tow, the tug was brought alongside HMS *Highflier*. Leading Seaman Davis and Able Seaman Stones immediately volunteered, and having been transferred by the tug to the burning *Musquash*, which had by this time broken adrift, they secured a line from her stern, by means of which she was towed into midstream. The line then parted, and Davis and Stones passed another line from the *Musquash* to the pumping-lighter *Lee*, which had now arrived. They then both went forward to the burning part, and succeeded in getting to the ammunition, which was by this time badly scorched, pulled it away from the flames and threw it overboard. They then broke open the door of the galley, which was on fire inside, to enable the *Lee* to play her hoses into it. They repeated the same thing with the cabin.

By their work they made it possible to subdue the fire and save further damage and loss of life. At any moment whilst they were on board the *Musquash* the ammunition might have exploded.' (LG 26th March 1918)

Captain T. K. Triggs was awarded posthumously the Albert Medal in Gold for this incident, whilst Leading Seaman T. N. Davis, Able Seamen R. Stones and W. Becker of HMS *Highflier* and A. C. Mattison and Able Seaman E. S. Beard of HMCS *Niobe* were all awarded

The burial at sea of Lt-Cdr T. N. Davis, GC, 7th November 1978.

41

the Albert Medal, which was posthumous to Mattison and Beard. Stone died soon after the explosion and Becker died in 1970.

After the First World War, Mr Davis spent sixteen years in China. He was married and had two sons and his hobbies were reading and music. He was a founder member of the Albert Medal Association.

He was recalled for the Second World War and rose to the rank of Lieutenant-Commander, serving in the Atlantic and North Africa theatres. He held the following campaign medals: 1914–15 Star, British War Medal, Victory Medal, 1939–45 Star, Atlantic Star, Africa Star, War Medal, Cadet Force Medal and Queen's Silver Jubilee Medal 1977.

Lieutenant-Commander Davis spent the last years of his life at Rhostryfan in Caernarvonshire, where he died on 8th October 1978, aged 83. His Albert Medal is now on display in the Museum, HMS *Dolphin*, Submarine Hard, Portsmouth.

Horace James CANNON, GC (formerly AM)

Flt Sgt H. Cannon, AM, RFC.

Horace Cannon, GC.

Horace James Cannon was born on 26th July 1895, the son of an army Sergeant. Horace's father first enlisted in 1873 and over a period of forty-three years, served in three campaigns before volunteering his services yet again during the First World War. During that war, he served as a Sergeant, finally retiring in 1918, in his sixty-third year – a remarkable record in itself.

Horace was educated at St Bede's Grammar School, Bradford, Yorkshire and volunteered his services on the outbreak of war in 1914. He joined the Royal Flying Corps, probably owing to his engineering background, and served in No 5 Training Squadron, remaining in the RFC throughout the war and attaining the rank of Flight Sergeant.

After the war, he returned to Bradford and owned his own business there, H. Cannon

Ltd, Motor Engineers and Car Sales. He and his wife, Emily, had four children; two boys and two girls. His hobbies were football and car rallies.

Recalled for service in 1939, Horace Cannon served with the Home Guard in the rank of Corporal. He died on 21st September 1975 and was cremated at Nab Wood Crematorium, Bradford.

In addition to the Albert Medal, Mr Cannon received the 1914 Star, British War and Victory Medals, together with the Defence Medal for service in the Home Guard. He was invested with the George Cross by Her Majesty Queen Elizabeth II on 18th July 1972.

The citation for the award of the Albert Medal is as follows:

'On 26th January last, while flying in England, a pilot when attempting to land lost control of his machine, which crashed to the ground from a height of about 150 feet, and burst into flames. Flight Sergeants Warne and Cannon went to the rescue of the pilot at great personal risk, as one tank of petrol blew up and another was on fire; moreover, the machine was equipped with a belt of live cartridges, which they dragged out of the flames. They managed to extricate the pilot, who was strapped to the burning plane, but he died shortly afterwards from his injuries and burns.' (LG 26th April 1918)

This action took place at Spittalgate Airfield, near Grantham and Flight Sergeant Albert Edgar Warne of 24th Wing Aeroplane Repair Section was also awarded the Albert Medal for his part in the rescue. Sadly, he was killed shortly afterwards by an aircraft propellor when starting up.

Horace Cannon's AM is now on display at the RAF Museum, Hendon; his GC is believed to have been sold at Sotheby's some years ago.

John George STANNERS, GC (formerly AM)

John George Stanners was born in September 1890. Nothing at all is known of his early life. He was married but widowed in 1959; it is not known whether he had any children.

John Stanners was a Deckhand in the Royal Naval Reserve when he won the Albert Medal – it is thought in Port of Spain, Trinidad.

'On the 29th December 1917, some cotton waste, which had been stored in a wooden cupboard in the magazine of HM Motor Launch No 289, caught fire from an unknown cause. On the fire being discovered by the smell of burning and by the issue of smoke from the magazine hatch, when opened, Deckhand Stanners, without hesitation, went down into the magazine and brought up a quantity of the burning waste.

John Stanners, AM.

43

Leading Deckhand Bugg, who was in Motor Launch No 285, alongside No 289, smelt something burning, and on observing Deckhand Stanners coming up from the magazine with burning material, immediately went down and extinguished the remainder of the ignited cotton waste.

The promptitude of action and the high courage shown by these men in the face of very grave danger averted a serious fire, and in all probability saved both Motor Launches and the lives of those on board.' (LG 21st May 1918)

Leading Deckhand Rupert Walter Bugg also received the Albert Medal for this incident.

Mr Stanners declined to exchange his Albert Medal. He died in Newcastle-upon-Tyne on 23rd February 1974.

Bernard George ELLIS, GC (formerly AM)

Bernard George Ellis was born in Surbiton, Surrey on 21st November 1890 and was married with a son and a daughter.

During the First World War, he served with 1st/5th Battalion, The Royal East Kent Regiment (The Buffs) and it was whilst in Mesopotamia in 1918 that he won his Albert Medal in the following circumstances:

Bernard Ellis, GC.

'Lieutenant Ellis, The Buffs, was with a party at Shahraban, in Mesopotamia, under instruction in the firing of rifle grenades. A volley was fired, but one of the grenades, owing to a defective cartridge, did not leave the rifle, but fell back into the barrel with the fuse burning. The firer lost his head and dropped the rifle and grenade in the trench, but Lieutenant Ellis, who was separated from the man by four other men in a narrow trench, at once forced his way past them and seized the rifle. Failing to extract the grenade, he dropped the rifle and placed his steel helmet over the grenade, which at once exploded, severely injuring him. There can be no doubt that his prompt and courageous action greatly minimized the force of the explosion and saved several men from death or severe injury.' (LG 18th July 1919)

He was invested with his medal by the King in 1919 and with his George Cross by the Queen on 8th November 1972. His Albert Medal is now on display in The Buffs' Museum at Canterbury.

Mr Ellis died at Letchworth, Hertfordshire, on 1st July 1979.

Arthur Gerald BAGOT, GC, DSC (formerly AM)

Arthur Gerald Bagot was born in Perth, Western Australia, on 26th April 1888, the son of a sheep station owner.

He was educated at St Peter's School Adelaide, South Australia and Geelong Church of England Grammar School, Corio, Victoria, Australia.

Prior to the First World War, Arthur Bagot had emigrated to Canada, where he was to remain, with the exception of his war service, until 1925.

He enlisted into the Royal Naval Volunteer Reserve (RNVR) from Canada in 1916 and sailed for England in September of that year. Subsequently, he served with distinction in the Motor Launch Division of the Dover Patrol until 1919–20. His promotions and appointments in the RNVR were as follows: Temporary Sub-Lieutenant, RNVR, HMS *Attentive III* additional for ML283, 2nd April 1917; Temporary Lieutenant RNVR, HMS *Attentive* additional for ML283, 10th September 1917; Temporary Lieutenant, RNVR, HMS *Attentive II* additional for ML239 in Command, 5th August 1919.

Lt A. G. Bagot, DSC, AM, in 1918.

Mr Bagot won the Distinguished Service Cross for gallantry in naval actions on the enemy-held ports of Zeebrugge and Ostende, while serving in ML283 (LG 23rd July 1918) and was also Mentioned in Despatches. He received the British War Medal and Victory Medal.

After demobilisation, Arthur Bagot returned to Canada, remaining there until 1952, when he went back to his birthplace in South Australia. Soon after this, he settled on a farming property (wheat and sheep) north of Perth, at Piawaning near Wongan Hills in Western Australia. There he lived until retirement in 1962.

Mr Bagot served in the Volunteer Defence Corps of the Australian Military Forces (AMF) on part-time war service and held the appointment of OC Wongan Hills Company VDC in the rank of Captain: his personal number being W.73103 and his period of service being from 28th July 1942 until 15th October 1945. He was placed on the Retired List (VDC) (Western Command) as from 16th October 1945.

In 1938, Arthur Bagot had married Noel Irene Harris: they had no children. His hobbies included matters related to agriculture and, in earlier years, almost all sports, especially cricket, football, athletics and rowing. After he retired, lawn bowls took up much of his time. In 1977, he was awarded the Queen's Silver Jubilee Medal. He died in Perth, Western Australia, on 21st November 1979.

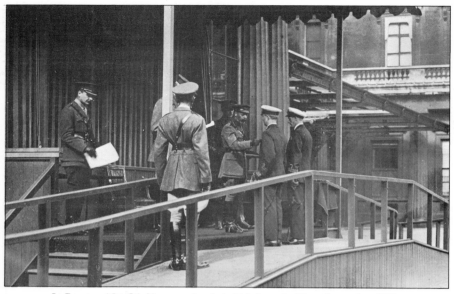

Lt Bagot and Lt-Cdr Hoare receive their AMs from the King, September, 1918.

ML239, an identical vessel to that in which Bagot won the AM.

The circumstances of the award of the Albert Medal to Arthur Gerald Bagot were as follows:

'On 12th April 1918, an explosion took place in the engine-room of HM Motor Launch 356, and the forward tanks burst into flame. The officer and some of the crew were blown overboard by the explosion, and the remainder were quickly driven aft by the flames, and were taken off in a skiff. By this time the flames were issuing from the cabin

46

hatch aft, and there was much petrol burning on the surface of the water. It was then realised by the crews of adjacent vessels that the aft petrol tanks and the depth charge were being attacked by the fire, and might explode at any moment. At the moment when others were running away. Lieutenant Hoare and Sub-Lieutenant Bagot jumped into their dinghy, rowed to the wreck, got on board, and removed the depth charge, thereby preventing an explosion which might have caused serious loss of life amongst the crowd of English and French sailors on the quay.' (LG 20th August 1918)

Lieutenant Keith Robin Hoare, DSO and Bar, DSC, RNVR, was also awarded the Albert Medal for this action.

Sidney WILLIAMS, GC (formerly AM)

Sidney Williams, AM, with his brother.

Sidney Williams was born in Lambeth, London, on 23rd December 1887. Before the First World War, he was an errand boy for Northcliffe Press at 6/- (30p) per week. He joined the Territorial Army before the war and when war broke out, he was with 6th City of London Rifles. He was married to Teresa (née Gilbert) and they had two sons and a daughter.

He won his Albert Medal in January 1918, endeavouring to rescue a friend of his, coincidentally also named Williams, but with a different Christian name – George.

'In France, on 4th January last, a soldier dropped a lighted match in a dug-out which had been used as a store for gunpowder. Although most of the gunpowder had been removed, there was a considerable amount scattered on the floor, which caught fire.

The soldier was overcome by the fumes, and in spite of the volumes of smoke issuing from the dug-out, Lance-Corporal Williams entered the dug-out and rescued the soldier, who was then badly burned and unconscious. Williams, who was severely burned, had to carry the man up twenty steps, and, if it had not been for his prompt action, the man would have lost his life.' (LG 30th August 1918)

Unfortunately, the rescued man died of his injuries four days later.

After the war, Mr Williams was a driver for *The Times* newspaper for forty years, with a clean driving record on his retirement. He served with the ARP (Air Raid Precautions) during the Second World War.

Sidney Williams was a Freemason and a Freeman of the City of London. He gave his

Sydney Williams, GC (centre).

Albert Medal to the Imperial War Museum, where it is now on display and was invested with the George Cross in 1972. Other medals he received were the 1914–15 Star, British War Medal and Victory Medal. He died in London, aged 87, on 12th October 1976.

Geoffrey RACKHAM, GC (formerly AM)

Geoffrey Rackham was born on 7th August 1896 and attended the Latimer School in North London. Nothing is known of his early years but he joined the Army Service Corps on 16th June 1915 and was commissioned on 23rd May 1917. He received the Albert Medal as a Second Lieutenant for great gallantry on 27th October 1918.

'At Le Cateau on the 27th October 1918, a lorry (one of a convoy of seven) laden with shells and cartridges caught fire. Lieutenant Rackham, who was awakened by the fire alarm, hurried to the scene of the fire in his pyjamas to find that flames three to four feet high were issuing from the petrol tank. He put the cap on the petrol tank, jumped into the driver's seat, started up the blazing lorry and drove it, while cartridges were exploding, to a place of safety, afterwards helping to extinguish the flames. By his prompt and courageous conduct, serious damage, and in all probability loss of life, was averted; for the other loaded lorries were close by, and some 130 men of the battery were only thirty yards distant.' (LG 3rd January 1919)

Mr Rackham was attached to 545th Siege Battery, Royal Garrison Artillery, at the time of his award.

Geoffrey Rackham was demobilised in the rank of Lieutenant on 24th November 1921. He was married to Dr Betty Scurfield and they had two daughters. His wife died in 1962. It is of some interest that Dr Scurfield's brother was Commander B. G. Scurfield, DSO, OBE, AM, RN, who won the Albert Medal in HMS *Hunter* in 1937. He was killed as a prisoner of war during a bombing raid in 1945.

After the war, Mr Rackham became a director of Shelvoke and Drewry at Letchworth, a firm which specialised (and still does) in building, among other vehicles, refuse collection lorries. He was subsequently managing director of his own municipal cleansing firm, also at Letchworth. He sold his business and retired in 1960. He was invested with his George Cross on 6th March 1973, having received the Albert Medal from King George V on 9th May 1919. This medal is now in the Museum of the Royal Corps of Transport, Aldershot.

Geoffrey Rackham became a founder member, with Commander David Evans (q.v.) of the Albert Medal Association in 1966 and he died on 10th January 1982, aged 85.

Lt G. Rackham, AM, RASC, about 1918.

Harry Melville Arbuthnot DAY, GC, DSO, OBE (formerly AM)

Harry Melville Arbuthnot Day was born on 3rd August 1898 in Sarawak, South East Asia, where his father was a member of the Sarawak Civil Service. He was educated at Haileybury College, joining the Royal Marines Light Infantry on 1st September 1916. Promoted Acting Lieutenant on 26th September 1917 and Lieutenant on the same date, he became a Captain on 1st September 1927, transferring to the Royal Air Force on 21st June 1930.

He won the Albert Medal two days before the end of the First World War for the following act of gallantry:

'On the 9th November 1918, HMS *Britannia* was torpedoed by an enemy submarine. The explosion of the torpedo was followed by another and more violent explosion of ammunition, and fires were started, resulting in the spread of smoke and fumes. Shortly after the explosion Lieutenant Day went down to the ward-room to search for wounded. He heard groaning forward of the ward-room, but found that the heavy wooden door leading forward had jammed and was immovable. He then burst open the trap hatch to the ward-room pantry and climbed through it. He discovered Engineer Lieutenant Stanley F. Weir, RN, and a ward-room steward alive and conscious, but unable to move. Fearing that he would hurt them if he endeavoured to drag them through the trap hatch single-handed, he climbed back into the ward-room aft and up on to the quarter-deck and procured two or three stokers, with whom he returned to the

Wg Cdr H. M. A. Day, AM, seated, third from right, Spangenberg, December 1939.

ward-room, eventually carried the dying officer and man on deck and to the forecastle. During his first visit to the ward-room Lieutenant Day was alone, in the dark, the ship with a list, and a fire close to the 12-inch magazine. Whilst carrying out this rescue work he inspected all scuttles and deadlights in the ward-room (and cabins before it) and ascertained that all were properly closed before leaving. The cordite fumes were very strong, and his life was in danger throughout.' (LG 7th January 1919)

Lieutenant Day was invested with his medal at Buckingham Palace by His Majesty King George V on 13th February 1919, only the third Royal Marine to be awarded the AM. In 1929, he led Hendon Air Show Synchronised Aerobatic Team (a forerunner of the Red Arrows). By the beginning of the Second World War, Day had risen to the rank of Wing Commander and whilst flying a Blenheim reconnaissance aircraft of 57

Gp Capt H. M. A. Day, GC, DSO, OBE.

50

'Wings' Day's decorations and medals being presented to the RM Museum, Portsmouth.

Squadron on 13th October 1939, he was shot down and remained a prisoner of war until 1944.

He was the leader of several escape organisations, including the mass breakout from Stalag Luft III in March 1944. The film 'The Great Escape' was based on this episode and 'Wings', as he was known, was portrayed in the film. He was recaptured three times and ended the war as one of thirteen special prisoners in the security wing of Sachsenhausen concentration camp, where he was manacled to the floor for a month, daily expecting execution. He is one of the few to be awarded the DSO for service whilst a prisoner of war (LG 28th December 1945). He also received the OBE (LG 28th December 1945).

After the war, he returned to duty and finished his service in 1950 as a Group Captain. He acted as Technical Adviser for the film 'Reach for the Sky'.

Married twice, he had two children, one of whom survived him. His hobbies included fishing, shooting and gardening.

Other medals held by Group Captain Day included the British War Medal, Victory Medal, 1939–45 Star, War Medal, Queen's Silver Jubilee Medal 1977 and Legion of Merit (USA). All his medals are now on display at the Royal Marines Museum at Eastney, Hampshire, including his original Albert Medal award.

'Wings' spent much time latterly in Malta, where he died, aged 79, on 2nd December 1977.

Harriet Elizabeth FRASER, GC (formerly AM)

Harriet Elizabeth Fraser was born in 1889. Little is known of her early life but she served as a Staff Nurse in the Territorial Force Nursing Service (TFNS) during the First World War

Above: a typical Casualty Clearing Station on the Western Front. Inset: Harriet Fraser, GC.

and in 1918, along with three other ladies, was awarded the Albert Medal in the following circumstances:

'Early in the morning of 1st October 1918, a serious fire occurred in No 36 Casualty Clearing Station at Rousbrigge in Belgium. At the time, some of the patients were undergoing serious operations in the abdominal and general operating theatres, the walls of which were composed of wood. The first intimation of danger in the theatres was the extinction of the electric light accompanied by volumes of smoke, and almost immediately the wooden walls burst into flames. The two sisters and staff nurse assisted in carrying the unconscious patients to safety, and returned to the burning wards to assist in carrying out other patients. During this time, ether bottles and nitrous oxide cylinders were continually exploding, filling the air with fumes and flying fragments of steel.' (LG 31st January 1919)

Sister Gertrude Walters Carlin, TFNS, who died as Mrs Dickinson, RRC, AM, at Gore, New Zealand on 9th April 1969 and Sister Gladys White, British Red Cross Society, who died in Southampton, together with Miss Alice Batt, VAD, were also awarded the Albert Medal for this incident.

After the war, Miss Fraser went to India, married Captain (later Colonel) S. J. Barry, RAMC in 1922 and they had two sons and a daughter. Colonel Barry died in 1959.

Like many of her fellow Albert Medal holders, increasing age and frailty precluded much active support for the Association but, like nearly all the others, Mrs Barry was a very keen moral supporter of the Association and its aims. She died at Guildford on 17th June 1980.

David Hywel EVANS, GC (formerly AM)

David Hywel Evans was born on 28th May 1898 at Llangefni, Anglesey, the son of the headmaster of Llangefni Grammar School, S. J. Evans, OBE, MA.

He was conscripted for service in the First World War in 1916 and was commissioned into the Royal Naval Volunteer Reserve. He was on board HMS *Trident* at Zeebrugge in April 1918 and it was as an officer on the same ship that he won his Albert Medal, in September 1918.

Cdr D. H. Evans, GC.

'On the 16th September 1918, a serious explosion occurred amidships on board HMS *Glatton* whilst lying in Dover Harbour. This was followed immediately by an outbreak of fire, the oil fuel burning furiously and spreading fore and aft. Efforts were made to extinguish the fire by means of salvage tugs. The foremost magazines were flooded but it was found impossible to get to the after magazine flooding positions. The explosion and fire cut off the after part of the ship, killing or seriously injuring all the officers who were on board with one exception. The ship might have blown up at any moment.

Lieutenant Belben, Sub-Lieutenant Evans, Petty Officer Stoker and Able Seaman Nunn were in boats which were rescuing men who had been blown, or who had jumped overboard. They proceeded on board HMS *Glatton* on their own initiative, and entered the superstructure, which was full of dense smoke, and proceeded down to the deck below.

Behaving with the greatest gallantry and contempt of danger, they succeeded in rescuing seven or eight badly injured men from the mess deck, in addition to fifteen whom they found and brought out from inside the superstructure.

This work was carried out before the arrival of any gas masks, and, though at one time they were driven out by the fire, they proceeded down again after the hoses had been played on the flames. They continued until all chances of rescuing others had passed, and she was ordered to be abandoned, when she was sunk by torpedo, as the fire was spreading, and it was impossible to flood the after magazines.' (LG 31st January 1919)

Lt David H. Evans, AM, RNVR, in 1924.

As a result of this action, twenty-three men were saved, eight by Mr Evans. As well as Evans, Lieutenant G. D. Belben, DSC, RN (DSO in 1944), PO A. E. Stoker and AB E. Nunn received the Albert Medal. Mr Evans was invested with his medal by the King at Buckingham Palace on 29th March 1919.

After the war, David Evans went to the University of Wales, Aberystwyth, graduating BSc in 1921. He then went to Oxford, taking his MA degree in 1923, afterwards becoming a master at Radley College from 1923-25.

He rejoined the Royal Navy in 1925, serving as an Instructor Officer until 1947, retiring as an Instructor-Commander. He married Marjorie Elisabeth Lea, LRAM, in 1932 and they had a daughter.

David Hywel Evans is remarkable in a unique way amongst those in these pages. He had strong feelings about what he considered was the reduced status of the AM and its recipients in the 1960s, and in 1965, he had a letter broadcast by the BBC programme 'Listening Post', appealing for surviving holders of the Albert Medal to contact him with a view to forming an Albert Medal Association from those surviving at that time. His first reply was from Geoffrey Rackham (q.v.) and by 1966 sufficient people had come forward to make the formation of an Association worthwhile. Widows of Albert Medal holders were eligible for Associate Membership of the Association. Commander Evans became Secretary of the Association, holding the post from 1966 until 1972, when he became a member of the VC and GC Association Committee.

It is quite apparent from just a cursory glance at the reams of notes in his small, spidery handwriting how much interest Commander Evans took in the Association he had been instrumental in forming and his concern for the welfare of all members of the Albert Medal Association, of which there were some 73 full members and 23 associates comes through most vividly. Many of the members and widows were even then aged and infirm.

He campaigned ceaselessly and tirelessly over the years for the recognition which he (and others) felt the Albert Medal was due, being rewarded in 1971 by the announcement on the exchanges. It was no understatement of the late Ross McWhirter, a stout champion of the cause and a friend of David Evans, when he said: 'The services of Commander Evans to those who at last enjoy the status of the George Cross are unsurpassed.'

It gives the author great pleasure to place David Evans' valuable and historic contribution to justice on record in these pages, since the original idea for this book was his also.

Commander Evans lived near Ripon in Yorkshire after his retirement. His Albert Medal is now on display in Llangefni Comprehensive School, Anglesey, North Wales and other medals awarded to him are the British War Medal, Victory Medal, 1939-45 Star, Altantic Star, Defence Medal War Medal and Queen's Silver Jubilee Medal 1977.

He died at his home on 8th December 1985, after a long illness, aged 87, as this book was being compiled.

Christopher FEETHAM GC (formerly AM)

Christopher Feetham was born on 25th December 1890. Little is known of his early life but at the age of 13, he started work in a nut and bolt factory at 2/9d (approximately 13p) per week. He then went to work in a rail factory before joining the Merchant Navy in 1908.

During his first voyage, he was involved in the Messina earthquake, for which he received the Messina Earthquake Medal and went on to serve in an American ship until the outbreak of war in 1914. He was torpedoed twice during the First World War before winning the Albert Medal in 1918.

'On the 10th November last, while the SS *Hornsey* was lying at Sunderland, a fire broke out in the mess-room and adjoining saloon. A quantity of ammunition was on board, and there was accordingly a great risk, if it exploded, of loss of life and property, as the effects of the explosion would probably not have been confined to the shipping in the harbour, but would have spread to the quay.

The whole of the ship's company behaved admirably in the emergency; and the Master, Chief Engineer, Second Mate, Steward and one of the Gunners did exceptionally well in their efforts to get the fire under control. The decisive factor, however, in extinguishing it and saving life and property was the heroism of Feetham. He volunteered to be let down into the cabin, and there, waist-high in water, he was able to direct his hose on to that part of the fire which would have exploded the ammunition in a very short time. As it was, some of the ammunition cases were already scorched.' (LG 18 March 1919)

Christopher Feetham, GC.

Mr Feetham was married and had six sons and six daughters. After the First World War, he worked on the compressors building the London Underground system and then went as a water diviner to a German firm.

During the Second World War, he helped to build Mulberry Harbour and the Thames Forts.

On 30th November 1972 he was invested with the George Cross. He died in Battersea, London, on 2nd October 1976. In addition to the GC, he held the British War Medal, Victory Medal and Mercantile Marine War Medal.

Randolph Gordon RIDLING, GC (formerly AM)

Randolph Gordon Ridling was born on 17th March 1888 at Auckland in New Zealand and attended the Richmond Road Primary and Auckland Grammar Schools. Subsequently, he went to Auckland University.

Enlisting in the New Zealand Rifle Brigade on 14th December 1915, he was eventually posted to Europe and it was as a Lieutenant in the NZRB in Staffordshire that he won the Albert Medal.

'At Brocton Camp, Stafford, on 19th April 1918, a recruit who was under instruction in bombing dropped a live Mills' grenade in the throwing bay after pulling the pin. Lacking the presence of mind to attempt to escape, he kicked the bomb towards the entrance and retreated to the inner end of the bay. Lieutenant Ridling, NZ Rifle Brigade, the bombing officer, seeing the man's danger, went to his rescue. Seizing him in his arms, he started to carry him out, but the bomb exploded before he could get clear of the bay, and he was wounded severely in the groin. But for Lieutenant Ridling's coolness and bravery the man, who was only slightly wounded, would, in all probability, have lost his life.' (LG 9th December 1919)

R. G. Ridling, GC, 1983.

He was demobilised as a Temporary Captain.

Randolph Ridling married Emily Shaw and they had a daughter. After the war, he attended Cambridge University (Queen's College), graduating in 1921 with an MA and Diploma in Agriculture. He returned to New Zealand and between 1922 and 1931, he was an Inspector with the Technical Branch of Taranaki Education Department. From 1931 to 1950, when he retired, he was a Director of Wellington Technical College.

Mr Ridling's hobbies were woodwork, gardening, walking and reading and besides the Albert Medal, which he elected to retain, he held the British War Medal, Victory Medal, 1935 Jubilee Medal and 1937 Coronation Medal.

He died in Wellington, New Zealand, on 13th January 1975, aged 86.

Walter Charles CLEALL, GC (formerly AM)

Walter Charles Cleall was born on 25th August 1896 and educated at Cardiff Elementary School. It is of interest that his Regular Army Certificate of Discharge (Army Book 108) gives his year of birth as 1896. His civilian employment was labourer.

He joined the Royal Welsh Fusiliers on 10th September 1914, serving throughout the war as a Drummer and being demobilised on 20th March 1919. It was whilst on demobilisation leave that he was awarded the Albert Medal, for rescuing Miss Winnie Jones, a hotel maid, from a fire.

'On August 11th a fire broke out at the top of the Royal Hotel Cardiff, and it was not until the sixth floor of the building was burning fiercely that one of the maids was seen to come to a window on that floor and gesticulate for help. Mr Cleall, who was in the crowd below watching the fire, at once entered the building without a smoke helmet, and eventually succeeded in getting to the sixth floor and into a room from which he could see the girl. From the window of that room he climbed along a narrow parapet, and reached the window where the girl was.

Above the ledge which afforded him a foothold was a stone balcony for a part of the intervening space, but a very dangerous corner had to be negotiated with a sheer drop to the street of fully one hundred feet. The risk of falling was very great, but he succeeded in carrying the girl back along the parapet, and into the room from which he started. A portion of the roof collapsed as the girl was assisted from the room.' (LG 30th December 1919)

Walter Cleall, GC.

Mr Cleall also received the Silver Medal of the Society for the Protection of Life from Fire for his gallantry.

On 2nd March 1920, he re-enlisted into the Welsh Guards with the number 2730560, where he spent the next seven years, transferring to the Reserve as a Lance-Corporal with a character assessment of 'Very Good'. His testimonial reads: 'Was a labourer before enlistment. Has a 2nd class certificate of education. Has proved a thoroughly trustworthy and reliable NCO. Clean, sober and hardworking.'

He spent a further five years on the Reserve, finally being released on 1st March 1932.

Walter Cleall was married – his wife's name was Annie-May – and they had a son and a daughter. He became a cabinet maker by trade later in life and was keen on rugby and swimming.

Apart from his Albert Medal, which he donated to the National Museum of Wales, Cardiff, at the time of the exchange, he had the 1914–15 Star, British War Medal, Victory Medal, Defence Medal and Queen's Silver Jubilee Medal 1977. Strangely, his Certificate of Discharge, written in 1927, makes no mention of the Albert Medal, although he had had it by this time for over seven years. One has the impression from what little one knows of Mr Cleall, that he was an exceedingly shy and modest man.

He died in hospital at Merthyr Tydfil on 27th April 1983, aged 86.

Edmund Geoffrey ABBOTT, GC (formerly AM)

Edmund Geoffrey Abbott was born on 20th July 1895 and educated at Bradfield Preparatory School, the Royal Naval College Osborne and the Royal Naval College Dart-

Left: Lt E. G. Abbott, AM, RN, leaves Buckingham Palace with his mother after his investiture in 1920. Right: Capt E. G. Abbott, GC, RN, with his family.

mouth. He spent four years at the two Royal Naval Colleges, joining HMS *Cumberland*, a training cruiser, as a Cadet in May 1912. During the First World War, he spent some months in the Dover Patrol, as a Sub-Lieutenant on HMS *Flirt*.

By April 1917, Abbott had become a Lieutenant. He was promoted Commander in 1926 and Captain in August 1939. His last appointment was as Captain i/c Simonstown and he retired at the top of the Captains' List in June 1948. He was Mentioned in Despatches in *The London Gazette* of 1st January 1942. Captain Abbott was present at the Penang Conference in September 1945 and his signature appears on the resultant document.

He fought in both world wars and was awarded the following campaign medals: 1914–15 Star, British War Medal, Victory Medal, 1939–45 Star, Africa Star, Burma Star, Defence Medal, War Medal, Jubilee Medal 1935 and Coronation Medal 1937. He exchanged his Albert Medal for the George Cross in 1972.

Captain Abbott's Albert Medal was awarded in the following circumstances:

'On the 5th August 1919, an explosion occurred on board the ex-German battleship *Baden*, whilst in dry dock at Invergordon. Lieutenant Abbott immediately proceeded down the hatch to the main deck and saw that smoke was coming from the ladder way tunnel leading down to the shaft passage and after room containing the cooling plant.

Other measures proving ineffectual, he proceeded to the corresponding tunnel on the starboard side, to see whether it was possible to get below and work up to the scene of the explosion from that side.

The starboard tunnel was practically clear of smoke, so he proceeded to the upper deck, collected a party, and descended again through the tunnel to the room containing the cooling plant. He made his way to the port side and found a dockyard workman lying unconscious. Assisted by the party which had accompanied him, Lieutenant Abbott got the body to the upper deck, but life was found to be extinct.

Although greatly affected by the fumes, Lieutenant Abbott called for further volunteers and again proceeded to the rescue of a second man whose groans had been heard, and succeeded in removing him out of danger.

Throughout the proceedings this officer showed an utter disregard for his own safety, and, in spite of the great difficulty occasioned by the absence of light, was the undoubted means of saving the second man's life.' (LG 12th March 1920)

The investiture was held by His Majesty King George V on 12th May 1920.

Captain Abbott was married twice and had two daughters by his first marriage and two sons by his second. He retired to Crowthorne in Berkshire, where he died on 3rd April 1974, aged 78.

Henry BUCKLE, GC, OBE (formerly AM)

Henry Buckle was born on 21st August 1889 and joined the Royal Navy in 1906, serving until retirement in 1934. However, he was recalled in 1939 and retired for the second time in 1946. From 1934 until 1939, he was a Whaling Inspector in the Antarctic, a job he returned to after the Second World War, until his final retirement in 1959.

He was married with one daughter, who now lives in New Zealand. Commander Buckle was a classmate of A. W. Newman (q.v.) on a Lieutenants' Course at the Royal Naval College, Greenwich. He won his Albert Medal as Mate on board HMS *Tiger* in the following circumstances:

Henry Buckle, GC.

'While HMS *Tiger* was undergoing repairs at Invergordon, on the 27th August 1919, two dockyard fitters and an able seaman were overcome by noxious gas in the hold of the ship, and Stoker Petty Officer Bailey, accompanied by a sick berth attendant, made an unsuccessful attempt at rescue. Both he and his companion had put on respirators, but found them useless. Mr Buckle, the officer of the watch, then arrived on the scene, and in spite of the grave risk to life, which it was now evident would be incurred by further attempts at rescue, immediately went down and succeeded in passing a rope round one of the men. This man was got out, but Mr Buckle was considerably affected by the gas, and could do nothing further.

Stoker Petty Officer Bailey, though suffering from the effects of his previous attempts, repeated the operation, and succeeded in getting the other two men out, but all efforts to restore them were futile.' (LG 27th April 1920)

Stoker Petty Officer Albert Victor Bailey also received the Albert Medal for this incident.

In addition to his Albert Medal, which he declined to exchange, Commander Buckle held the OBE.

He was invested by His Majesty King George V on 22nd March 1922. He died at Pimperne, near Blandford Forum, Dorset, on 22nd January 1975, aged 85.

Jack CHALMERS, GC (formerly AM)

Jack Chalmers was born in Wellington, New Zealand, on 11th March 1894 and educated at Mosman Superior Public School. His family moved to Australia in 1906.

When the First World War began, he joined 47th Australian Infantry Battalion, Australian Imperial Force (AIF) and while in London in 1917, he married Jessie Alice Courtney, a Dorset girl. They were married for fifty-one years, until her death in 1968, and had a daughter.

Mr Chalmers was a keen surfer, being a member of North Bondi Surfing Life Saving Club, which he joined on 27th August 1919, obtaining his Bronze Medallion on 11th January 1920. He won many awards and saved many lives, becoming something of a legend in Australia. He won the annual SLS carnival in 1920–21 and it was in the following year, when competing in the same carnival, that the drama was to take place which would win for Jack Chalmers the highest civilian award for gallantry.

Jack Chalmers, GC, March 1973.

'On 4th February 1922, Milton Coughlan was swimming just outside the breakers at Coogee Beach, Sydney, N.S. Wales, when he was attacked by a shark, which bit deeply into his left forearm. Freeing himself, he fought and drove away the shark, which, however, returned and succeeded in establishing a hold on his right arm, but the grip was again broken.

Observing what had happened, Jack Chalmers had a line tied round his waist, and

61

immediately dashed across the rocks to the rescue, and although he slipped and fell, and was momentarily stunned through his head coming into contact with a rock, he quickly recovered, plunged into the water and swam out to Coughlan, who was floating helplessly in the water; Chalmers caught hold of him round the body, and held him until they were both hauled in to the rocks.

The injured bather's arms were practically bitten through and the flesh torn from them, and the unfortunate man succumbed to his injuries shortly after reaching hospital.

Jack Chalmers undoubtedly fully realised the risk he was incurring and showed extraordinary gallantry in going to Coughlan's rescue in the circumstances. That the danger was considerable is clear from the fact that a number of sharks were seen swimming around the spot where the rescue occurred immediately after the bather was lifted ashore.' (LG 7th July 1922)

Jack Chalmers served in the Second World War and held the Queen's Silver Jubilee Medal 1977. He died on 29th March 1982, aged 88.

Richard Walter RICHARDS, GC (formerly AM)

Richard Walter Richards was born on 14th November 1893 in Bendigo, Victoria, Australia. He took a science degree at Melbourne University and answered an advertisement for a physicist to go on the Shackleton Trans-Antarctic Expedition of 1914–17, sailing at two weeks' notice.

It was whilst on this expedition that he won the Albert Medal for a gallant rescue under most arduous conditions.

'The Expedition had for its object the crossing of the Antarctic Continent from the Weddell Sea to the Ross Sea, via the South Pole, a distance of about seventeen hundred miles. Sufficient supplies for the journey could not be carried, and it was therefore necessary to establish a chain of depots on the Ross Sea side as far southwards as possible. With this end in view the ship *Aurora* was sent to McMurdo Sound at the southern extremity of the Ross Sea and, as it was intended that the vessel should winter there, a portion only of the stores and equipment was disembarked. McMurdo Sound was reached in January 1915, but during a blizzard in May, the *Aurora* was blown out to sea and was unable to return, and the nine members of the Expedition who were on shore were left stranded. They recognised that failure to establish the depots would undoubtedly result in the loss of the main body and resolved, in spite of their grave shortage of equipment to carry out the allotted programme.

For this purpose a party under the command of Sub-Lieutenant A. L. Mackintosh, RNR, and consisting of the Reverend A. P. Spencer-Smith, Messrs Joyce, Richards, Hayward and Wild and three other members who assisted for a part of the outward journey left Hut Point, Ross Island, on October 9th. They took with them two sledges and four dogs, and 162 days elapsed before the surviving members of the party were back at Hut Point, the total distance covered being approximately 950 miles.

Mr Spencer-Smith had to be dragged on a sledge for forty-two days, mainly by hand labour, the distance covered being over 350 miles. When more than 100 miles remained

R. W. Richards, GC, and his wife.

to be covered the collapse of Lieutenant Mackintosh imposed an additional burden on the active members of the party who were all suffering from scurvy and snow blindness and were so enfeebled by their labours that at times they were unable to cover more than two or three miles in fifteen hours. Mr Spencer-Smith died when only nineteen miles remained to be covered, but Lieutenant Mackintosh was brought in safety to the base.' (LG 6th July and 2nd May 1924)

Ex-PO E. E. M. Joyce, Victor George Hayward (then deceased) and PO H. E. Wild, RN, (then deceased) also received the Albert Medal for this incident.

Mr Richards was married and had two sons and one daughter. His first wife died in 1972 and he remarried in January 1974. He presented his Albert Medal to the Antarctic Department of the Australian Government. He also held the Polar Medal with bar for 1917, one of only seven awarded, and received the Jubilee Medal in 1977.

On his return from the Antarctic, Mr Richards became an instructor in mathematics and physics at the Ballarat School of Mines, becoming principal in 1945, until his retirement in 1959. An annual award to the best student at Ballarat School of Mines is the Richard Walter Richards Medal. He was the author of *The Ross Sea Shore Party*, published by the Scott Polar Research Institute, Cambridge.

Mr Richards died in Victoria, NSW, Australia, on 8th May 1985.

Stanley Frederick GIBBS, GC (formerly AM)

Stanley Gibbs was born at Hunter's Hill, Sydney, Australia, on 2nd January 1909. For most of his life he was employed by the Gas Light Company at Sydney. He met his wife, Doris Mannix, there and married her in September 1948. They have no children.

He received the Albert Medal for gallantry attempting to save the life of a bather from a shark.

'On the 3rd January 1927, at Port Hacking near Sydney, New South Wales, a youth named Mervyn Allum was swimming a short distance from the shore when he was attacked by a large shark. It was at first thought that he was drowning, and Stanley Gibbs, who was standing on the nose of a launch he was driving, ready to give assistance to Allum, observed that he was being attacked by the shark. Gibbs dived from the launch and fought the shark with his hands and feet and eventually succeeded in getting Allum, who was very badly injured, from the jaws of the shark, and with the assistance of a man named Macdonald placed him in a rowing boat. The victim died of injuries shortly afterwards.' (LG 8th February 1927)

S. F. Gibbs, GC, 1973.

Stanley Gibbs was invested with his Albert Medal at Sydney Town Hall on 28th March 1927 by the Duke of York (later HM King George VI). When the Second World War broke out, he was enlisted into the army, joining 35th Battalion, with whom he saw action in New Guinea.

He retired in 1974 and enjoys lawn bowls for recreation. He was awarded the Queen's Silver Jubilee Medal in 1977.

George Stewart BAIN SMITH, GC (formerly AM)

George Stewart Bain Smith was born on 1st December 1898 at Grampound, near Truro, in Cornwall, the eldest son of Captain Henry Feather Smith and his wife, Evaline Mary, daughter of Donald Bain, JP, of Keynsham, near Bristol. He was intended for the Royal Navy and commenced to sit the Osborne entry exam of 1911. In the middle of that exam, he was seen to have measles, so was told to leave the exam room. In those days, such an irregularity could prove fatal to an examinee's aspirations. His father, who had taught both the Prince of Wales and the Duke of York to play golf, appealed directly to King George V but to no avail. Young Bain Smith was therefore sent off to Blundell's School to prepare for entry to the RMA Woolwich, which was successful and he was commissioned into the Royal Artillery as a Second Lieutenant on 6th June 1918.

Bain Smith's time at Woolwich, according to him, was principally distinguished by designing and building a new and inventive howitzer, which he demonstrated by

Capt G. S. Bain Smith, AM, RA. Lt-Col G. S. Bain Smith, GC.

demolishing the Commandant's greenhouse! Eleven days after being commissioned, he was in action in France and a week later, he was in command of his battery, since the battery was hit, killing all the other officers. Surviving the war intact, despite being shot down from an observation balloon, he was sent out to Mesopotamia and was involved in relief operations during the Arab revolt. At the end of that, he was employed with the Indian Army as a Mountain Gunner.

In 1924, he subsequently was employed with the Indian Army Ordnance Corps. He married at Simla, India, in 1925, Gertrude Hilda Eileen, eldest daughter of Lieutenant-Colonel Roger Lewis Campbell Sweeney, DSO, OBE, MC, (brother of Archbishop James Fielding Sweeney of Toronto), a distinguished officer who died shortly afterwards. After his marriage, he was on leave in England during the General Strike and to return he commandeered the 'Bristolian' express at Bristol and drove it, with a naval stoker, to London. His enthusiasm affected his control of the throttle somewhat and he missed the stop at Reading by half a mile! At Paddington, which he entered with more care, he was given a clap by the passengers, so he must have arrived safely.

Back in London, he mounted two expeditions to the Himalayas and explored Gilgit and Little Tibet, including the supposedly impassable Silk Route from Leh in the area now disputed by China. He recorded the latter expedition on ciné film, which is still held by the family. It was during one of these expeditions that Bain Smith won the Albert Medal for a spectacular rescue.

'On the 3rd June, Major Minchinton, with two Gurkha companions, was descending an ice slope on a mountain in the Himalayas when at a height of about 14,000 feet the party lost their foothold and slid or fell some 1,000 feet on to a snow slope below. Major Minchinton and one of his companions were so badly injured that they were unable to move, but the third managed to make his way to Lakka, some 3,000 feet lower, where at 2.30 pm he met and informed Mr Bain Smith of the accident. Mr Bain Smith, though he had no knowledge or experience of mountaineering, at once set out with a coolie to rescue Major Minchinton from his position which he reached at 4.30 pm after a climb of 3,000 feet. Mr Bain Smith had no ice axe and was wearing smooth-soled boots and he could only proceed across the snow field by kicking footholds in the hard snow with his stockinged feet. The coolie who had accompanied Mr Bain Smith from Lakka was unable to cross the snow and remained behind. On reaching Major Minchinton, Mr Bain Smith made of his coat a sledge and accompanied by the Gurkha who was just able to move, proceeded to drag the injured man over the freezing snow to a point some 500 feet lower. Further progress without assistance was impossible and Mr Bain Smith therefore descended alone across the snow slope until, after a journey of about a mile, he met with two shepherds who accompanied him back to where the injured man lay. Major Minchinton was lowered a further 500 feet until descent was checked by the roughness of the snow. Mr Bain Smith thereupon made a second journey and after great difficulty found four shepherds whom he sent back to Major Minchinton. He himself was by that time so exhausted that he could only proceed by crawling. He found Major Minchinton struggling and his struggles were such that, as the snow had frozen hard, he could not be moved. Mr Bain Smith, after sending the injured Gurkha down with two of the men, made repeated but unsuccessful efforts to continue the descent. At sunset the remaining shepherds deserted him.

Mr Bain Smith, who was clad only in a shirt, shorts and stockings, stayed for half an hour with Major Minchinton who was then unconscious, if not already dead. An ice cold wind was blowing and there were occasional hailstorms and it was obvious that nobody left exposed on the slope would survive the night. Mr Bain Smith, after covering Major Minchinton with his coat, descended to a fire that was seen burning below the glacier where he found Mrs Minchinton and a party of men, none of whom were capable of tackling the mountainside in the dark. The first rescue party arrived at 3 am on the following morning, and Mr Bain Smith escorted them to a point whence Major Minchinton's body could be seen. He was then on the verge of collapse and both feet were frost-bitten.' (LG 30th September 1927)

Colonel Bain Smith wrote and contributed photographs for *The Times of India*. In India, he was for a while Commodore of the Indus Yacht Club and Secretary to the Himalayan Ski Club.

In 1936 or 1937, he was invalided home with tuberculosis and sent to Switzerland to recuperate. Despite his illness, he skied there and recorded on film some of the Olympic winter sports. He never returned to India but was sent to Aldershot, where he fitted out the Brigade of Guards for the British Expeditionary Force. At that time, he had the honour of being presented to King George VI. It seems that equipment for the BEF was so short that bicycle capes had to be commandeered from Halfords, for gas capes, and lavatory paper (the old-fashioned hard type) for message pads. It appears that the Guards looked a fine sight in their Halfords capes!

By 1940, his tuberculosis was so bad, he had a lung and a half removed at Midhurst and was invalided out. After a short and successful recuperation, he was offered and accepted the job of Bursar at Sedbergh School, in about 1941. He subsequently became Chairman of the

Bursars' Association and retired in about 1961, remaining for some time Financial Advisor to Sedbergh School and a member of Lord Peel's Outward Bound organisation. His health finally gave way and after three heart attacks and continuing pulmonary trouble, he died at his home in Cartmel, near Grange-over-Sands in Cumbria on 22nd January 1972.

He was a talented photographer, a keen skier and sailor. Of a practical turn of mind, he designed and built his own caravan with which, in the late 1940s, the family toured the Highlands. He also built a boat in which they sailed on Lake Windermere. He contributed to several publications, including *The Caravan*. He was a member of the Davos Association. He sketched well but was never still long enough to take art seriously. A good shot and horseman, he disliked game shooting, preferring to use a camera. He was a point-to-pointer in India, when he could afford a suitable mount.

Mrs Bain Smith died a short time after her husband, leaving two sons, one of whom has kindly written the substance of the foregoing account.

Colonel Bain Smith's Albert Medal is now in the collection of the Royal Artillery at Woolwich and in addition to his George Cross, he was awarded the British War Medal, Victory Medal, General Service Medal with clasp 'Iraq', India General Service Medal 1908 with clasp 'North West Frontier 1935' and War Medal 1939–45. He also held the Life Saving Medal of the Order of St John.

John FAIRCLOUGH, GC (formerly AM)

John Fairclough was born at St Helens, Lancashire, on 29th October 1900, the son of William Henry Fairclough, a glassworks manager, and his wife, Mary Ann Fairclough. There were eight sisters and one brother, besides himself. Educated locally, he went to work at the United Glass Works, St Helens, where his father was manager, when he left school.

At the age of 19, John Fairclough enlisted for seven years into the Royal Garrison Artillery, the whole of which he spent in India – it is thought at Lucknow. Whilst in India, he enjoyed horseriding.

He won the Albert Medal as Gunner 1424030, whilst serving with 21st Medium Battery, Royal Artillery, in 1927.

'On the night of the 27th April, 1927, a serious fire occurred in a godown in Ambala. Three Indian boys had gone to the godown in a lorry to get petrol and they entered the building carrying a lantern. The naked light ignited the petrol vapour with which in the hot weather the building was filled and in a very short time the whole building was ablaze. On the outbreak of the fire the lorry driver departed and before any organised aid could arise the boys were trapped in the burning building. Gunner Fairclough who happened to be walking alone near by at once went to their assistance. In spite of the fact that the heat from the burning building was so intense as to keep onlookers at a considerable distance from the fire, he three times entered the building and rescued the three children. Gunner Fairclough was severely burned and unfortunately the three Indian boys later died.

Gunner Fairclough in entering on three separate occasions a burning building containing a highly inflammable and in certain circumstances a highly explosive substance, three times put his life in the gravest danger. To enter the building the first

Left: John Fairclough, GC. Right: Gunner John Fairclough, AM, taken about 1928.
The cross-belt is artistic licence as he was never commissioned.

time was an act calling for great courage, but to enter it twice thereafter, knowing the full danger to be run, was an act of exceptional gallantry.' (LG 8th May 1928)

Gunner John Fairclough received his award from the Viceroy.

On his return to St Helens after his army service had expired, he met Miss Elizabeth Ann Barber and married her on Christmas Eve 1931. They had three children, all daughters: between them, there were nine grandchildren and ten great-grandchildren.

Mr Fairclough was re-engaged by United Glass upon his return and he worked there until his retirement in 1965. He became blind shortly thereafter.

He was called up for service in the Second World War at the age of 41 but was declared medically unfit, presumably as a result of his brave act in India many years before, and spent the war working in the glass works.

When offered the opportunity to exchange his Albert Medal for the George Cross, John Fairclough declined as he was not one for 'a fuss' and it was only after his death that many of his workmates learned of

John Fairclough, GC, in 1965 at Salisbury.

his gallantry award. Presumably also due to his reticence, he also declined membership of the VC and GC Association, being, it is believed the only Albert Medallist to do so, although he did belong to the Albert Medal Association.

Mr Fairclough was awarded the Queen's Silver Jubilee Medal in 1977 and died at St Helens on 12th October 1984.

Reginald William ARMYTAGE, GC, CBE (formerly AM)
Dick OLIVER, GC, BEM (formerly AM)

'On the 23rd May 1928, whilst HMS *Warspite* was lying alongside Parlatorio Wharf, Malta, an examination of the bulge compartments situated on the port side aft was being carried out. The manhole door of the lower bulge compartment was removed and the compartment tested. It was found that the air was foul and poisonous. A Chief Stoker attempted to enter the compartment, although aware that it was in a dangerous condition, and was immediately overcome by the gas and fell unconscious to the bottom of the compartment, a distance of about 20 feet.

The alarm was given and Lieutenant Armytage immediately fetched his gas mask and with a life line round him entered the compartment and reached the bottom, when he was overcome and rendered unconscious. With great difficulty, owing to the small size of the manhole, he was hauled to the exit by means of the life line. He was unconscious and had stopped breathing when hauled into the open air, and was eventually removed to the RN Hospital

Lt R. W. Armytage, AM, RN, at the time of his award.

in a precarious condition. Lieutenant Armytage was aware that his gas mask would afford no degree of protection against the CO or CO_2 gases likely to be present in the compartment. He realised that the delay incurred in passing a diver through the manholes would probably prove fatal to the Chief Stoker and appreciated to the fullest extent the grave risk he ran in entering the compartment.

As soon as Lieutenant Armytage had been withdrawn from the manhole of the upper bulge compartment Leading Seaman Oliver, who was in attendance with a shallow diving helmet volunteered to attempt the rescue of the Chief Stoker, despite the fact

Left: CPO Dick Oliver, AM, and his wife at Portsmouth during the Second World War.
Right: Dick Oliver, GC, BEM, with his wife.

that he had witnessed the painful and distressing sights attendant on asphyxiation. After donning the helmet he was passed with considerable difficulty through the manholes of the upper and lower bulge compartments and he eventually succeeded in reaching the Chief Stoker and passing a line round his body by means of which the latter was drawn up through the manhole to the pontoon abreast the ship. On emerging from the bulges Oliver was a very bad colour and suffering to some extent from the poisonous gases in the bulge compartments. Although a smoke helmet provides a considerable degree of protection it was obvious that any displacement would be attended by serious results and, further, having regard to the difficulty in passing Oliver through the manholes when equipped with the helmet, it was quite clear that his quick withdrawal in the event of being overcome was a matter of considerable conjecture, and the delay thus involved might have been attended with fatal results. (LG 3rd August 1928)

Reginald William Armytage was born on 18th May 1903. He won the Albert Medal with Dick Oliver (q.v.) as a Lieutenant RN on board HMS *Warspite* in 1928, as related above. Lieutenant Louis Mountbatten was a staff officer on *Warspite* at the time.

Admiral Armytage held the CBE (LG 1st January 1959), Defence Medal, War Medal, Coronation Medal 1953 and Jubilee Medal 1977, in addition to the Albert Medal, which he declined to exchange.

He held a number of senior appointments in the Royal Navy, including those of: Head of Gun Design and Senior Navy Representative at Armament Design Establishment, 1946; Deputy Chief Inspector of Naval Ordnance, 1949; Chief Inspector, 1956. He was also Vice-President (Naval) Ordnance Board, 1959 and President in 1961.

On retirement, he and his wife went to live in Downton, near Salisbury, in Wiltshire, where he died, aged 81, on 9th November 1984.

Dick Oliver was born on 6th August 1901 at Christchurch and went to Christchurch School from 1906 to 1913. In January 1916, he joined the Royal Navy, serving for nearly thirty years until 1946, retiring as a Chief Petty Officer. His Albert Medal was awarded for his services as outlined above.

He was invested with the AM by His Royal Highness the Prince of Wales on 28th March 1929, as the King was then convalescing at Bognor.

Dick Oliver retired to Dorset with his wife, Eileen, (née Day) and they were married for over fifty-five years. They had no children.

In addition to the Albert Medal, which he elected to retain, Mr Oliver held the British War Medal, Victory Medal, 1939–45 Star, France and Germany Star, Defence Medal, War Medal, Queen's Silver Jubilee Medal 1977 and the Naval Long Service and Good Conduct Medal. His hobbies, when younger, included rowing, shooting and athletics but in latter years, he concentrated on gardening. Mr Oliver died on 5th February 1986.

Alexander Henry MAXWELL-HYSLOP, GC (formerly AM)

Alexander Henry Maxwell-Hyslop was born on 25th May 1895 and was educated at a day school at Dover and Rottingdean School, near Brighton, from 1905 to July 1907, when he entered Osborne. He remained there until 1910, when he went to Dartmouth until 1913. Serving throughout the First World War, he began the war as a Midshipman on HMS *Centurion* and served on RNA Station Polegate, Sussex, HMS *Africa*, HMS *Repulse*, and HMS *Revenge* before the end of the war, by which time he was a Lieutenant.

Further promotion and appointments followed and by 1929, he was a Lieutenant-Commander, serving as a Gunnery Officer on board HMS *Devonshire*. In July of that year, there was a serious explosion on board, as a result of which two Albert Medals and two Empire Gallantry Medals were awarded.

Capt G. C. Maxwell-Hyslop, GC, RN, escorts King George VI on board HMS *Cumberland* in 1942.

'HMS *Devonshire* was carrying out full calibre firing on 26th July 1929, when at the first salvo there was a heavy explosion which blew off the roof of one of the turrets.

Marine Streams was the only man in the gun house who was not either killed instantly or fatally injured. He was seriously shaken by the explosion and instinctively

71

climbed to the top of the side plating to escape but, on arriving at the top he looked back and saw the conditions inside the turret, and deliberately climbed back into it amidst the smoke and fumes notwithstanding the grave risk of further explosions. He then helped to evacuate the one remaining man of the right gun's crew, and took charge and played a major part in evacuating the crew of the Fire Control cabinet. When all the wounded were out he collapsed. His bravery, initiative and devotion to duty were beyond praise.

Lieutenant-Commander Maxwell-Hyslop was in the fore control when the explosion occurred, and immediately proceeded to the turret and climbed inside. He made a general examination of the turret, and descended the gun well through most dangerous conditions of fumes and smoke, necessitating the use of a life line, remaining in the turret until the emergency was over, directing arrangements for the safety of the magazine, and supervising the evacuation of the wounded. He was fully aware of the danger to himself from the results of cordite fumes, and the grave risk of further explosions.

At the time this officer and man entered the turret the fire produced by the explosion was still burning and it was impossible to estimate the real state of affairs due to the heavy smoke. They both were fully aware that there were other cordite charges in the hoist and handling room below which might ignite at any moment with almost certain fatal results to themselves, and they deliberately endangered their own lives to save the lives of others.' (LG 19th November 1929)

Marine Albert Edward Streams (PO.21038) was also awarded the AM for this incident. Streams was Maxwell-Hyslop's personal wardroom attendant and they remained friends until Streams' death in action in Sicily in 1943. His medals were stolen from his widow's home at Reading in 1966.

Midshipman A. J. Cobham (now Commander Cobham, GC) and the late Able Seaman G. P. Niven, GC, were awarded the Empire Gallantry Medal for this incident.

Lieutenant-Commander Maxwell-Hyslop went on to serve with the Royal Navy until July 1946, holding a variety of appointments, retiring as a Captain. He was an Aide de Camp to King George VI in 1944–45.

In addition to his Albert Medal, Captain Maxwell-Hyslop held the 1914–15 Star, British War Medal, Victory Medal, 1939–45 Star, Atlantic Star, Africa Star, War Medal (with Mention in Despatches), Jubilee Medal 1935 and Jubilee Medal 1977. He was married to Cecelia Joan (née Bayly) and they had two sons, one of whom, Robin Maxwell-Hyslop, is Conservative Member of Parliament for Tiverton, Devon.

On retirement, Captain Maxwell-Hyslop went to live in Cornwall, where he farmed near Par. His Albert Medal is now on display at HMS *Excellent*, Portsmouth. He died on 28th August 1978, aged 83.

Robert Murray KAVANAUGH, GC (formerly AM)

Robert Kavanaugh was born at Wingham, New South Wales, on 18th December 1906. He attended Randwick High School in Sydney and went on to Sydney University, to graduate as a dentist.

In 1929, he performed an act of gallantry which was to result in the award of the Albert Medal.

'On the evening of the 12th January 1929, Colin J. Stewart a boy of 14 years of age, was bathing at Bondi Beach, New South Wales, some fifty yards from the shore, when he was attacked by a shark which inflicted serious injuries to his right side and hip. Robert Murray Kavanaugh, aged 22 years, of Darlinghurst, New South Wales, who was bathing some few yards from Stewart, without hesitation swam to his assistance and had almost reached him when the shark made a second attack on Stewart. Undeterred by the danger to himself, Kavanaugh secured hold of Stewart and struggled with him towards the shore. He had gone a considerable distance when he was met by two other men and together they carried Stewart to the beach, where he was given medical attention and then conveyed to hospital. Stewart, however, succumbed to his injuries the following morning.' (LG 30th October 1930)

Robert Kavanaugh, GC.

On 12th April 1933, Robert Kavanaugh married Mary Potter and they had three daughters and a son. During the Second World War, he was stationed as a dentist with the RAAF at Bathurst Island.

In 1957, Mr Kavanaugh bought a sheep property called 'Karalinga' near Wollondilly, New South Wales, while at the same time maintaining his dental practice at Bowral, NSW, until his retirement in 1972. He died on 12th November 1976, his wife having died shortly before him.

Florence Alice ALLEN, GC (formerly AM)

Florence Alice Allen's Albert Medal was one of the decorations awarded for the terrible Quetta earthquake in May 1935. No less than eight Albert Medals and nine Empire Gallantry Medals were awarded for gallantry during this disaster, ten of the recipients subsequently converting their medals to the George Cross.

Miss Allen was born on 26th September 1906 and spent her early years on Ascension Island. She was educated privately on Ascension and then in England at the Royal Marines School at Chatham. After leaving school, she trained as a nurse in Halifax, Yorkshire. She worked for some time as a children's escort between the United Kingdom and India between

The devastation following the Quetta earthquake.

the wars and at the time of her award was nurse to Christopher, the son of Flight Lieutenant C. H. Turner, RAF, of No 5 (AC) Squadron, RAF Quetta.

Her Albert Medal citation reads as follows:

Florence Alice Allen, GC.

> 'At the risk of her life, and at the cost of terrible injuries to her leg, Miss Allen saved the life of the child in her charge by throwing herself across the cot. She has displayed the highest courage ever since.' (LG 19th November 1935)

Florence Allen married a man with the same surname when she was 40. They had one daughter, Jillian Maria but sadly, Mrs Allen's husband died of pneumonia a week after the birth of their child. After the death of her husband, Mrs Allen took up children's nursing again with families.

She received the Queen's Silver Jubilee Medal in 1977 and made national headlines in 1982, when she was attacked and robbed in her own home by two youths, who stole £25. They were later caught and sentenced.

After suffering for many years the after-effects of her 1935 injuries, Florence Allen died, aged 78, on 1st August 1985.

Interestingly, she mislaid her Albert Medal but despite this, she was still invested with the

George Cross. However, her medal is one of two exchange awards known to have found their way into private hands (*vide* Bryson). Miss Allen was invested with her original award by His Majesty King Edward VIII in the only investiture to be held during his short reign.

Sir John Guise COWLEY, GC, KBE, CB (formerly AM)

John Guise Cowley was born on 20th August 1905 in Dorchester, Dorset, the son of the Reverend Henry Guise Beatson Cowley. Educated at Wellington College and the Royal Military Academy, Woolwich, he was commissioned into the Royal Engineers as a Second Lieutenant in 1925. Promotion to Captain followed in 1936; Lieutenant-Colonel in 1941; Brigadier in 1943; Major-General in 1953 and finally Lieutenant-General in 1957. During the Second World War, he served in the Middle East, Italy and North West Europe, being appointed an OBE (LG 18th February 1943) and Mentioned in Despatches four times. He was appointed CBE in 1946 (LG 1st January 1946)

Several senior appointments followed the end of the war: Chief of Staff Headquarters Eastern Command 1953–56; Vice-Quartermaster General 1956–57; Controller of Munitions, Ministry of Supply 1957–60 and Master-General of the Ordnance 1960–62. He retired from the army in 1962 but held the appointments of Colonel Commandant Royal Pioneer Corps from 1961–67 and Colonel Commandant Royal Engineers 1961–70. He was created CB in 1954 and KBE in 1958. He is a Knight of the Order of Orange Nassau.

General Cowley was married to Irene Sybil Millen in 1941 and has a son and three daughters. After his retirement from the army, he held the Chairmanship of Bowmakers from 1963 to 1973 and Keith & Henderson Limited. He was the Chairman of the Albert

Lt-Gen Sir John G. Cowley, GC, KBE, CB.

Medal Association from 1966 to 1972. He was also a Governor of Wellington College and a Director of British Oxygen.

His army postings included Woolwich, Chatham, Aldershot, Bangalore, Quetta, US Staff College as an instructor and Germany. In addition to his other decorations mentioned above, Sir John holds the 1939–45 Star, Africa Star, Italy Star, France and Germany Star, Defence Medal, War Medal, and Queen's Silver Jubilee Medal 1977.

He was invested with his Albert Medal by King Edward VIII on 14th July 1936, that monarch's only investiture and upon exchanging his AM for the George Cross, Sir John gave his original medal to Wellington College for display.

Like Florence Allen (q.v.), General Cowley won his Albert Medal for gallantry in the Quetta earthquake.

'Lieutenant Cowley and his party were the first to start relief work at the Civil Hospital where the walls of all the wards had collapsed bringing down the roofs intact on the inmates on whom the debris of the walls had already fallen. At first the men were too few in number to tear off the roofs, so they raised them up for short periods whilst Lieutenant Cowley crawled under them and dragged out survivors from their beds. The survivors were pre-earthquake hospital patients and mostly quite helpless. Lieutenant Cowley lifted many men in his arms regardless of the warning that they were suffering from all manner of diseases. Had it not been for the work of this officer and the excellent example shown by him to his men, very many less men would have been saved alive.' (LG 19th November 1935)

Sir John was serving with the 16th Army Troops Company, Queen Victoria's Own Madras Sappers and Miners.

He now lives quietly in retirement in Hampshire.

Robert SPOORS, GC, MM (formerly AM)

Robert Spoors was born on 11th July 1910. Little is known about his early life. He joined the West Yorkshire Regiment in 1926 and served with them until medically discharged as a Sergeant in 1942. He and his wife, Jane, had a son and a daughter.

He was at Quetta in 1935 during the terrible earthquake in May of that year and was one of the resulting eight Albert Medallists.

'After the earthquake on the morning of 31st May, Private Spoors, at very considerable risk to himself from falling debris, entered Major O'Hanlon's house which was in a dangerous condition. He was successful in clearing a path for Mrs O'Hanlon and was mainly responsible for saving her life. He then re-entered the house to save the nurse and baby, but was himself caught in the debris and was later rescued by two other men and brought out in an exhausted condition. He subsequently worked for long hours at the British Military Hospital. His action was reported by the Colonel Commanding the Hospital with a recommendation for special recognition; the facts being corroborated by Major O'Hanlon, RAMC. Private Spoors' gallant behaviour and devotion to duty were most praiseworthy.' (LG 19th November 1935)

The group of eight medals awarded to Private Roberts Spoors, GC, MM.

Mr Spoors served in Palestine before the Second World War and was awarded the MM for bravery (LG 22nd December 1939). His interest was sport, especially boxing and he served the Royal British Legion as Pensions Officer for the Forest

Inset: Robert Spoors, GC, MM.

Men of the West Yorkshire Regiment searching the ruins after the Quetta earthquake 1935.

Hall Branch during the 1950s. He was a foreman engineer from 1943 to 1972.

His Albert Medal is now in the Regimental Museum of the West Yorkshire Regiment and as well as the GC, he held the General Service Medal with clasp 'Palestine', 1939–45 Star, Africa Star, Defence Medal, War Medal and Queen's Silver Jubilee Medal 1977. His GC, MM and other medals were sold at Christie's in November 1985.

Robert Spoors died in Norwich on 28th February 1984, aged 73.

William Simpson McALONEY, GC, OBE, (formerly AM)

William Simpson McAloney was born on 12th May 1910 in Adelaide, Australia and educated at Thebarton Public School and the Adelaide School of Mines. He was service representative for the South Australia Tractor Company from June 1928 until June 1931 and a garage and engineering workshop proprietor from July 1931 to June 1936, where he remained until he joined the Royal Australian Air Force on 1st July 1936. He served with them until retirement on 11th May 1967. In the RAAF he studied navigation, Morse code, bombing and pyrotechnics, besides part-time training as an air gunner. He was an Aircraftman Aero Engine Fitter when he won the Albert Medal for the following act of extreme gallantry:

Photograph taken at the RAAF Base at Laverton in mid 1937, showing the actual Hawker Demon Aircraft A1-31, which crashed at the static air display of the Hamilton Royal Show on 31st August 1937. In front of the aircraft, left to right: Flying Officer McKenzie (Pilot), Sergeant N. Torrenswitherow (Observer Gunner) – both these men lost their lives in the crash. Aircraftman McAloney is on the right of the picture.

78

Bill McAloney as a Flight Lieutenant in the Second World War, wearing the ribbon on his uniform of the original Albert Medal awarded to him for his heroism. Right: McAloney as he is today – the only holder of the George Cross in the RAAF.

'For conspicuous gallantry in attempting to rescue an officer from the burning wreckage of an aircraft at Hamilton, Victoria, on 31st August 1937.

Despite the fact that the aircraft was ablaze from nose to rudder, Aircraftman McAloney dashed into the flames and continued his efforts at rescue until pulled away in an unconscious condition, having received severe burns which necessitated his removal to hospital'. (LG 18th February 1938)

A rare document from that time is a copy of the actual recommendation to the Prime Minister, dated 23rd November 1937, that McAloney should receive the Albert Medal for his exploit.

Group Captain McAloney served during the Second World War as a Flight Lieutenant and saw action in Dutch New Guinea. In the 1960 Queen's Birthday Honours List, Group Captain McAloney was appointed OBE for his work with the Aircraft Research and Development Unit and the operation of the first Mirage fighter.

He was married in 1935 to Dora Winifred Johnson and they had four daughters and three sons, one of whom was awarded the Military Cross in Vietnam.

In addition to his GC and OBE, Group Captain McAloney also holds the 1939–45 Star, General Service Medal with clasp 'Malaya' and Silver Jubilee Medal 1977. He now lives in Victoria, Australia.

Alfred MILES, GC (formerly AM)

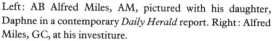
Left: AB Alfred Miles, AM, pictured with his daughter, Daphne in a contemporary *Daily Herald* report. Right: Alfred Miles, GC, at his investiture.

Alfred Miles was born on 12th June 1899 in London but nothing is known of his early life.

He served as an AB with the Royal Navy during the last war and won the Albert Medal in December 1940 rescuing a shipmate.

'On 1st December 1940, when HMS *Saltash* was passing from one dock basin to another, a wire was run out from the starboard bow to the weather corner of the gate so as to hold the bow up to the wind. The wire was taken to the windlass, but this was too slow, and men were picking up the slack by hand, leaving some loose turns on the deck. As the ship drew level the order was passed to turn up. The wire was taken from the windlass to the bollards. Able Seaman Miles saw Able Seaman Thompson standing in a bight of wire and called out to him to get clear, but he failed to do so and the wire drew taut round his ankles. Miles knew that Thompson might be hauled through the bull-ring and that if he himself were caught in the wire he would be in the same danger; yet he tried to force the bight open with his hands. His right hand was jammed between the wire and Thompson's foot. He said nothing and still tried to

A fine portrait of Alfred Miles, GC.

free his shipmate. The hurt which caused the loss of his hand was not known until later. Thompson was dragged along the deck to the bull-ring but way was taken off the ship just in time to save him.' (LG 29th April 1940)

The Albert Medal in this case has a rather unusual inscription upon it, *viz*: 'Awarded by The King for Gallantry in risking his life and losing his right hand to save a shipmate in HMS SALTASH on 1st December 1940'.

Mr Miles was invested in August 1941 by the King at Buckingham Palace and his AM is now on display in the National Maritime Museum.

Alfred Miles was married with two daughters but is now a widower. He is a keen photographer and was a founder member of the Albert Medal Association.

He served in the Navy in both world wars. A regular sailor, he held the 1914–15 Star, British War Medal, Victory Medal, 1939–45 Star, Atlantic Star, Defence Medal, War Medal, Silver Jubilee Medal 1977 and Naval Long Service and Good Conduct Medal. He now lives in Kent.

John Henry MITCHELL, GC, BEM (formerly AM)

John Henry Mitchell was born on 1st January 1917. Nothing is known of his early life but he served in the Royal Naval Reserve from 1939 to 1946, being commissioned in 1941. As an officer, he served in HMT *Minuet*, HMS *Myosotis*, HMS *Leander* for twenty months as a Gunnery Officer then First Lieutenant (Gunnery) of HMS *Sussex* in the Far East, finally serving on board HMS *Cumberland* for the passage home. He refused a permanent commission.

It was as an Acting Second Hand that he won the Albert Medal for the following act of heroism:

John Mitchell, GC, BEM, is second from left, front row, (behind Geoffrey Rackham).

'On 27th September 1940, Chief Engineman Wedderburn fell into the sea between two trawlers in harbour. He could not swim, and was soon unconscious. An unknown seaman, who jumped in to save him was soon in difficulties. Mitchell, hearing his shouts, clambered over a vessel to the quay, ran 100 yards, climbed across two other ships and jumped into the water. He seized Wedderburn, who was sinking, by the hair, and held up the other man until a rope was passed down from the trawler. This he secured with a bowline round the now helpless seaman, using one hand, while he supported both men and himself by gripping the rope with his teeth. The seaman was then hauled out of the water by the men in the trawler. Mitchell, although fully clad, and wearing seaboots, supported Wedderburn by treading water until a pilot ladder could be lowered. He made the rope fast round Wedderburn, and steadied him as he was hauled out. He had been in very cold water for thirty-five minutes, and was unconscious when rescued.' (LG 29th April 1940)

After the war, Mr Mitchell, who was demobilised as a Lieutenant-Commander, joined the Metropolitan Police, rising to Detective Inspector in Dept C10 (the Stolen Car Squad). He was awarded the British Empire Medal in the New Year Honours List of 1970.

Mr Mitchell was married with a son and a daughter and lived in West Norwood, London, until his early death of coronary thrombosis on 12th April 1972.

His Albert Medal is now in the Imperial War Museum.

David George Montagu HAY, GC (formerly AM) (later 12th Marquis of Tweeddale)

David George Montagu Hay was born at Gifford, East Lothian, Scotland, on 25th October 1921 and educated at St David's School, Reigate and Eton College. He was the nephew of the 11th Marquis of Tweeddale, whom he succeeded on the death of his uncle in 1967.

David Hay joined the Merchant Navy as a Cadet in 1939 and it was while serving on SS *Eurylochus* in the Atlantic in 1941 that he won his Albert Medal.

'Cadet Hay was serving in a merchantman which was sunk by an enemy raider. She was heavily shelled and machine-gunned, and many of her crew were killed. Two boats got away, but the others were shot to pieces. Those of the crew who were left on board launched two rafts, and just before the ship went down they jumped

David Hay, GC, Marquis of Tweeddale, pictured in May 1978.

in and swam for them. Cadet Hay reached a raft, but, although sharks were swimming all round him, he dived in again and rescued the Radio Officer. As he swam back to the raft his clothing was torn by a shark.' (LG 8th July 1941)

He subsequently became a Lieutenant in the Royal Naval Reserve, being demobilised in 1948. Married twice, his first wife was Sonia Peake, daughter of the 1st Viscount Ingleby, whom he married in 1946. They had three sons, two of whom were twins and were divorced in 1958. In 1959, he married Miss Nella Doreen Dutton, by whom he had two more sons, also twins. The Marquis suffered an uncommon allergy to bee and wasp stings called anaphilactic shock, which, since it could prove rapidly fatal, meant that an antidote always had to be at hand.

He declined to exchange his Albert Medal and held, in addition, the 1939–45 Star, Atlantic Star, Africa Star, Defence Medal, War Medal, the Queen's Silver Jubilee Medal 1977, Lloyd's War Medal for Bravery at Sea and a Royal Life Saving Society Medal. His hobbies were fishing and the study of wildlife.

Although he lived for a time on a 4,000-acre estate on the Isle of Mull, two years before he died, he moved back to the family estate at Gifford, East Lothian, where he died, aged only 57, on 23rd January 1979.

The Marquis of Tweeddale is so far the only holder of the George Cross to sit in either House of Parliament.

Albert HOWARTH, GC (formerly AM)

Albert Howarth was born on 10th May 1917 in Nelson, Lancashire and educated at Bradshaw Street Junior School and Bentley Street Senior School. He worked all his life in the cotton industry, save for war service in the Royal Navy between 1939 and 1942. He was married with two sons.

On 9th December 1940, Ordinary Seaman Albert Howarth, RN, was a member of the crew of HMS *Foresight* on a Malta convoy when he won his Albert Medal.

Albert Howarth, GC, proudly displays his original award.

'Ordinary Seaman Howarth was one of a boat's crew sent to board a burning and abandoned merchantman. The merchantman blew up as they drew near her, throwing the boat's crew into the water. Ordinary Seaman Howarth saw near him a Stoker who was badly shaken, so he held him up for ten minutes until a lifebelt was thrown to him. This he put round the Stoker, and before being hauled on board his ship, made sure that his shipmate was safe. When he himself reached the deck, after nearly half an hour in the water, it was seen that his right foot had been blown off.' (LG 2nd September 1941)

Mr Howarth was invalided out of the Royal Navy and was presented with his Albert Medal at Buckingham Palace by the King in 1942. He also held the 1939–45 Star, Atlantic Star and War Medal. An interesting sidelight is that he apparently first learned of his award through a children's comic, whilst he was in hospital recovering from his injury. The action was featured in the comic *Film Fun* in 1942, under the title 'Our War Heroes'.

Mr Howarth was invested with the George Cross on 5th December 1972 and gave his AM to the Townley Hall Museum, Burnley. His hobbies were do-it-yourself and gardening and he was Chairman of the Burnley Branch of the British Legless Ex-Servicemen's Association (BLESMA). He died at Burnley on 13th June 1976.

John Edward GIBBONS, GC, DSC (formerly AM)

John Edward Gibbons was born at Burnham, Buckinghamshire, on 26th April 1905. His family had been Quakers for generations and he was educated at a Quaker school, Sidcot. Nothing is known of his early life; his first wife died either shortly before the Second World War or early on in the war. He married his second wife, Maria Nimmo, the daughter of a prominent citizen of the island of Ischia in May 1946. There were two daughters of his first marriage and three daughters and a son by the second.

Commander Gibbons fought in a number of theatres during the war and held, in addition to the Albert Medal, the 1939–45 Star, Atlantic Star, Africa Star Italy Star and War Medal. He was Mentioned in Despatches and awarded the DSC in 1943 (LG 4th May 1943) for his part in the Allied Forces landings in North Africa. He won the AM as a Temporary Lieutenant RNVR in 1942.

'When a motor launch was mined her Commanding Officer was wounded in the head, and blown into the sea. He was rescued and went at once to save others. He saw a seaman some 100 yards away in the water, and swam to him through burning fuel. His gallant action helped to save the man's life.' (LG 11th August 1942)

Commander Gibbons was the Naval Officer in Command, Ischia, from 27th October 1943 until 27th February 1945. He was an Honorary Freeman of Ischia.

Lt-Cdr J. E. Gibbons, AM, RN (centre), in 1944 at Ischia.

After some five post-war years spent in salvage operations off Malta and a spell in the film industry, the Gibbons family went to South Africa in 1954. John Gibbons practised as an irrigation engineer until his death in 1971. After his death, his widow scattered his ashes at sea, just outside the port of Ischia, as he had loved the islands from the time he served there during the war.

Commander Gibbons died on 12th November 1971, three weeks after the exchange announcement was made. Although he is considered to be a George Cross holder, his family retained his Albert Medal. He died in Johannesburg, South Africa.

Charles Henry WALKER, GC (formerly AM)

Charles Henry Walker was born at Portsmouth, Hampshire, on 9th March 1914. Nothing is known of his early life; however, he became a regular member of the Royal Navy and it was as a Petty Officer Cook that he won the Albert Medal, on the Malta convoys in 1942.

Charles Henry Walker, GC.

'During a convoy to Malta a vessel was hit by bombs in an air attack and burst into flames fore and aft. An escorting destroyer went very close, lowered her whaler and picked up survivors from the sea. Petty Officer Cook Walker seeing a man in difficulties dived over the destroyer's side and rescued him. The heat was intense and he knew that his ship might have to turn away at any moment. Both rescued and rescuer were picked up.' (LG 15th December 1942)

Mr Walker subsequently paid tribute to the gallantry of an unknown Merchant Navy Officer who was clinging to the ratlines of a lifeboat with his one hand, his other arm having been blown off. He refused to be hauled into the boat which was already over-full. A drowning shipmate nearby caught his attention. He swam away to help him and was never seen again.

Charles Walker was invested with his Albert Medal by the King at Buckingham Palace on 13th August 1943. After retiring from the Royal Navy he became a postman in Portsmouth.

He received his GC on 12th March 1973 and donated his AM to the Victory Museum, Portsmouth Dockyard. Mr Walker also has the Naval General Service Medal with clasp 'Palestine', 1939–45 Star, Atlantic Star, Africa Star, Italy Star, War Medal, Silver Jubilee Medal 1977 and Naval Long Service and Good Conduct Medal. He is married and lives in Portsmouth. He was a founder member of the Albert Medal Association in 1966.

William GOAD, GC (formerly AM)

William Goad was born in Cambridgeshire on 10th May 1922. He went to school at Stretham, near Ely and joined the Royal Navy at 15 years of age. He served for sixteen years, retiring in 1953 as a Chief Petty Officer.

From that date, Mr Goad has been a farmer in Cambridgeshire with his brother. He is married and has three sons.

It was as a Leading Seaman on the Arctic convoys in 1942 that Mr Goad won his Albert Medal.

CPO William Goad, AM, 1946.

'Leading Seaman Goad went over his ship's side, on a line in water well below freezing point, and rescued an unconscious man. It was blowing a full gale and there was a very great risk that he would either be washed away by the breaking seas, or swept under the bilge keel of his ship, which was rolling heavily.' (LG 26th January 1943)

He was invested in July 1943 at Buckingham Palace by the King, together with thirteen other crew members of HMS *Ashanti*. Mr Goad also has the 1939–45 Star, Atlantic Star, Burma Star, Africa Star, War Medal, Korea Medal, UN Korea Medal, Naval Long Service and Good Conduct Medal and the Queen's Silver Jubilee Medal 1977.

On 21st November 1956, a new naval housing estate was opened by the Duchess of Kent in Darget's Wood, Chatham. Five VCs and 4 AMs of Nore Command had streets named after them, one of which is Goad Avenue. Mr Goad elected to retain his original award.

John Sedgwick GREGSON, GC (formerly AM)

John Gregson was born on 4th January 1924 in Bombay, India. His father was an architect in private practice. Educated in England, he attended the Pangbourne Nautical College in Berkshire, before commencing an apprenticeship with the Blue Funnel Line of Liverpool, in the general cargo trade.

As an Apprentice on the Malta convoy of August 1942, he won the Albert Medal while serving on board the MV *Deucalion*.

'The ship was set on fire by the explosion of a torpedo during an attack by enemy aircraft. The flames spread rapidly and almost immediately orders were given to abandon ship. One of the ship's gunners, however, was pinned under a raft. Apprentice Gregson immediately went to his assistance and, with help freed him. The gunner had

86

sustained severe injuries and, as it was impossible to get him into a boat or on to a raft, he was dropped overboard. Gregson dived into the sea after him, and, in the darkness, towed his helpless shipmate to a ship which picked them up, a distance of about 600 yards. But for Apprentice Gregson's gallant and determined action, undertaken with complete disregard of his personal safety, the injured man would have had little chance of survival.' (LG 2nd February 1943)

In 1943, Mr Gregson obtained his Second Mate's Certificate and from then until 1946 served as Third Mate and Second Mate with the Brocklebank Line. In 1946, he obtained his First Mate's Certificate. From 1946 to 1949, he was Second Mate and First Mate with Common Brothers Ltd, of Newcastle. In 1949, he obtained his Master's Certificate

John S. Gregson, GC.

and between that year and 1952 served as a Second Officer with the Orient Line.

In 1953, he settled in New Zealand, married his wife, Mary Joan, and had two sons.

Between 1953 and 1961, he served as Chief Officer, then Master, in coastal shipping with the Shell Oil Company of New Zealand. In 1961, he joined the Bay of Plenty Harbour Board as a Pilot in the port of Tauranga and in 1977 left there to return to sea-going duties as a Navigating Officer with the Union Steamship Company of New Zealand.

Mr Gregson declined to surrender his Albert Medal and also holds the 1939–45 Star, Atlantic Star, Africa Star, Burma Star, War Medal, Queen's Silver Jubilee Medal 1977 and the Lloyd's War Medal for Bravery in Saving Life at Sea.

James Arthur REEVES, GC (formerly AM)

James Arthur Reeves was born at Darwen in Lancashire on 15th June 1911. After a general education, he commenced a seafaring career in the Merchant Navy as an Indentured Apprentice with Manchester Liners in 1929, trading solely between the United Kingdom, Canada and the United States. He served as a Third Officer with the same company after obtaining his Second Mate's Certificate in 1934, when he gained his First Mate's Certificate and transferred to the Prince Line to obtain wider experience trading worldwide.

On return to the UK in 1939 and qualifying as Master Mariner in March 1940, he joined the Athel Line, a subsidiary of United Molasses Co Ltd, as Second Officer, intending to stay for only six months to gain tanker experience. Later that year he was promoted to Chief Officer and served in that rank for the remainder of the war, during which many Athel Line vessels were lost owing to enemy action. In April 1942, when serving on MV *Atheltemplar* in convoy PQ14 to North Russia, he survived several near misses from air and submarine attacks and completed the voyage to Murmansk and return to the UK. It was on the return voyage that HMS *Edinburgh* was lost whilst shadowing the convoy.

After repairs to the *Atheltemplar*, the vessel was again ordered to North Russia with a cargo of fuel oil in convoy PQ18 in September 1942. Although about seventeen ships were lost, including the *Atheltemplar*, this convoy was considered to be the turning point in the war as far as convoys to North Russia were concerned.

When the *Atheltemplar* was torpedoed in the engine room on 14th September 1942, Mr Reeves rescued two crew members from the flooded and destroyed engine room for which he was awarded the Albert Medal. The following citation appeared in *The London Gazette*:

Capt J. A. Reeves, AM, MN, Deputy Chairman, Albert Medal Association, shows his AM to Mrs Hansi Sunter, who did much secretarial work for the Association.

Capt J. A. Reeves, GC, at his reinvestiture on 6th March 1973; with him are his wife and brother. Reproduced by courtesy of the *Lancashire Evening Telegraph*.

'The ship was torpedoed and was being abandoned when two men were seen floating in the oily water which flooded the engine-room to a depth of 25 feet. Both were helpless, one being badly injured and the other overcome by oil fumes. All the engine-room ladders had been destroyed but using a boat ladder, Chief Officer Reeves descended into the engine-room and secured lines about both men. While being hauled to safety, one of the men slipped back into the oily water. Mr Reeves again descended into the engine-room which was rapidly filling with surging oil and water, and secured another rope about the injured man who was then brought on deck.

In descending into the darkened and flooded engine-room, Mr Reeves showed great personal bravery and complete disregard of his personal safety. His work was rendered doubly dangerous by the heavy oil fumes which had accumulated.' (LG 25th May 1943)

Mr Reeves was also awarded the Lloyd's War Medal for Gallantry for the same incident.

After the war, the Athel Line fleet was slowly rebuilt and Captain Reeves took command early in 1949 but he had to retire from the sea in 1962, due to ill health.

In February 1941, James Reeves married Eileen Gregory, daughter of Alderman John Gregory of Whitehall, Darwen, who was also Mayor of Darwen from 1938 to 1941. They had no children.

Whilst serving at sea, Captain Reeves' hobby was cabinet making and there were several small pieces of teak furniture made by him in his home in Darwen.

After retiring from the sea in 1962, he took up a minor post with Crown Paints at Darwen until he retired completely in 1976. In 1962, he accepted the post as District Commissioner for Boy Scouts in Darwen until 1967, when he was made Assistant County Commissioner until resigning in 1969.

On his retirement from Crown Paints in 1976, he became a committee member of the Darwen Civic Society and in 1977 was made an honorary member of the Rotary Club of Darwen. He took an active part in both these organisations. He also became a member of the Darwen Branch of the Royal British Legion and as a Service Secretary, attended to the requirements of needy service widows and servicemen by obtaining grants from the RBL HQ and attending to their Social Security entitlements where required. He was a member of the Probus Club, where he gave several talks on his experiences at sea but mostly confined to peace time.

Captain Reeves was invested with the George Cross on 6th March 1973, having received his Albert Medal on 24th May 1944. The Albert Medal was subsequently presented to the Athel Line for display at their Head Office in Knightsbridge. After the AM was translated to the GC, he was appointed a member of the VC and GC Association Committee (having been Deputy Secretary of the Albert Medal Association) in 1974 but had to resign in 1976, owing to the distance to travel to attend meetings in London.

He died on 26th December 1984, aged 73.

Eynon HAWKINS, GC (formerly AM)

Eynon Hawkins was born at Llanharan, South Wales, on 27th June 1920. Educated at the Llanharan Primary School he left there in 1934, at the age of 14, to work in the coal mines, where he remained until the Second World War.

AB E. Hawkins, AM, in 1940.   Eynon Hawkins, GC.

In 1940 he joined the Royal Navy, spending ten weeks training at HMS *Raleigh* and HMS *Drake*, before being drafted to a trawler patrolling the English Channel for nine months. Transferring as a Seaman Gunner to the DEMS (Defensively Equipped Merchant Ships), he served on several ships in the Atlantic, Mediterranean, Indian Ocean and Bay of Bengal. He was torpedoed whilst serving aboard the oil tanker MV *British Dominion*, in convoy of fourteen merchant ships from the West Indies to Malta in the Atlantic.

Mr Hawkins won the Albert Medal for Gallantry in Saving Life at Sea while a member of the crew of HMS *Chrysanthemum* in 1943. In addition to the AM, he also holds the Lloyds' Medal for Bravery and the Queen's Silver Jubilee Medal 1977.

After the war, in 1947, Eynon Hawkins became a professional rugby player, having already played for Llanharan, Bridgend and Glamorgan. In that year, after becoming professional, he played for Salford, Rochdale Hornets and Belle Vue. He won six Welsh International Caps for Rugby League.

The citation for the Albert Medal, which was presented by the King at Buckingham Palace on 16th November 1943, reads as follows:

'Able Seaman Hawkins was serving in a Merchant Vessel which was hit by three torpedoes and immediately began to burn furiously. Many of the crew jumped over-board and Able Seaman Hawkins, with the greatest coolness and courage, organised a party of survivors in the water and kept them away from the fire until they were later picked up by one of HM ships. Twice he swam to the assistance of other survivors who were in difficulties, himself receiving burns in the face as he pulled them to safety.' (LG 29th June 1943)

Eynon Hawkins returned to live in Wales in 1956 and worked underground until his retirement in 1980. He was invested with the George Cross by the Queen on 5th December

1972 and had the honour of being the last Albert Medallist to head the list of precedence at an investiture, as no VC was to be awarded. He was a founder member of the Albert Medal Association (now incorporated into the VC and GC Association) and his medal is on display at the National Museum of Wales, to whom it was presented in 1977.

William Henry Debonnaire McCARTHY, GC (formerly AM)

William Henry Debonnaire McCarthy was born on 2nd April 1911 but nothing is known of his early life and education.

He won the Albert Medal in 1943 for gallantry at sea off the coast of North Africa.

Cdr W. H. D. McCarthy, GC.

'Mr McCarthy dived into a tempestuous sea from the Mole at Benghazi to save some Indian seamen who had been thrown into the sea from a raft. When a line was thrown he swam with it to the Indians, caught hold of one of them and successfully brought him ashore. He then returned to the rescue of another. There was grave danger that Mr McCarthy would be dashed against the rocks by the gale and the high sea.' (LG 27 July 1943)

Mr McCarthy was subsequently commissioned and rose to the rank of Lieutenant-Commander. He was awarded the Queen's Silver Jubilee Medal in 1977 and died at Portsmouth, Hampshire, on 21st July 1978.

Gordon Love BASTIAN, GC, MBE (formerly AM)

Gordon Love Bastian was born in Barry, South Wales, on 30th March 1902. Educated at Barry High Street Elementary School, he enrolled on 2nd July 1981 to serve five years Indentured Apprenticeship at the Barry Graving Dock and Engineering Company. He joined the Merchant Navy and on 3rd August 1927, and took his Certificate of Competency of the British Board of Trade at Cardiff Marine Engineering Academy.

Mr Bastian served in the Second World War and took part as a Merchantman in the Battle of the Atlantic. Appointed an MBE in 1943 (LG 4th January 1943) he also received the Lloyd's War Medal for Bravery at Sea in 1944. He was invalided out of the Merchant Navy in 1943 as a Second Engineer Officer.

In addition to the decorations already mentioned, Mr Bastian holds the 1939–45 Star, Atlantic Star, War Medal and Queen's Silver Jubilee Medal 1977. He is married and has a son and a daughter. He has lived in Montreal since 1947.

Left: Gordon Love Bastian, MBE, AM, in the uniform of a Chief Officer, Merchant Navy, from the painting by Bernard Hailstone in the Imperial War Museum. Right: G. L. Bastian, GC, MBE, receives his GC from the Governor-General of Canada.

Gordon Bastian was serving on the *Empire Bowman* when he won his Albert Medal – coincidentally on his birthday. The ship was about 500 miles from Brest, in France, when it was torpedoed by a German submarine.

'The ship in which Mr Bastian was serving was torpedoed and sustained severe damage. Mr Bastian was on watch in the engine room when the ship was struck. He at once shut off the engines. He then remembered that two firemen were on watch in the stokehold. The engine room was in darkness and water was already pouring into it. Although there was grave risk of disastrous flooding in opening the watertight door between the stokehold and engine room, Mr Bastian did not hesitate but groped his way to the door and opened it. The two firemen were swept into the engine room with the inrush of water. One man had a broken arm and injured feet and the other was badly bruised and shaken. Mr Bastian made efforts to hold them both but lost one, so he dragged the other to the escape ladder and helped him on deck. He then returned for the other and helped him to safety. The more seriously injured man had practically to be lifted up the ladder by Mr Bastian, who was himself half choked by cordite fumes.

Second Engineer Officer Bastian took a very great risk in opening the watertight door into the already flooded and darkened engine room of the sinking ship and both men undoubtedly owe their lives to his exceptional bravery, strength and presence of mind.' (LG 17th August 1943)

Mr Bastian was invested with the George Cross by the Governor-General of Canada in the Governor-General's railway carriage on 27th November 1973 and he presented his Albert Medal to the National Museum of Wales, Cardiff, where it is now on display. His portrait by Bernard Hailstone is at the Imperial War Museum.

Geoffrey RILEY, GC (formerly AM)

Geoffrey Riley was born in Huddersfield on 20th November 1929 and educated at Holme Valley Grammar School. He went to Huddersfield Technical College from 1947 to 1954 and 1956 to 1960, the interruption being due to National Service in the Royal Air Force, in which he served as a Junior Technician.

On leaving school, he took up an apprenticeship with the Central Electricity Generating Board and after his studies at the Huddersfield Technical College, he obtained the Higher National Certificate with Endorsements. In later years he became a Member of the Institution of Electrical Engineers and a Chartered Engineer. All his working life has been spent with the CEGB, working in a number of Yorkshire power stations.

Mr Riley has lived all his life in the beautiful Holme Valley, an area at the foot of the Pennines, now well known to television viewers through the programme 'Last of the Summer Wine', which was filmed around Holmfirth.

Geoffrey Riley, GC.

He married a local girl in 1953 and they have two children; a son and a daughter. Since 1966, the family has lived in a large Victorian house with an acre of garden; the Rileys are keen gardeners. His other interests are do-it-yourself and restoration of vintage motorcycles. He hopes to be able to get more involved in local affairs in due course but finds this difficult owing to shift work. The family enjoys touring the continent by caravan and Mr Riley says that one of the pleasures of recent years has been the biannual reunions of the VC and GC Association, where he and his wife have made many friends.

Geoffrey Riley won the Albert Medal as a schoolboy in 1944 in the following circumstances:

'On the 29th May 1944, a thunderstorm, followed by a cloudburst, broke over the Digley Valley, near Holmfirth, Yorkshire, and the river Holme became a raging torrent eighty feet wide and over fifteen feet deep, flooding surrounding land and buildings. Geoffrey Riley, aged 14, saw that an elderly woman, aged 76, had taken refuge on a low wall, surrounded by flood water which was rising rapidly. He first attempted a rescue by walking to her along the wall, but she would not leave her position. He then entered the flood water, rescued her from the wall, which later collapsed, and, though only a moderate swimmer, struggled to bring her to safety through the flood until he became exhausted. His father Donald Riley went to his assistance, but all three were swept away into the river, Geoffrey Riley being the sole survivor.' (LG 3rd October 1944)

Mr Riley lives near Huddersfield, Yorkshire and he presented his Albert Medal for display to the Tolson Memorial Museum, Ravensknowle Park, Huddersfield.

Philip Robert Stephen MAY, GC (formerly AM)

Philip May was born on 6th August 1922 at Canterbury, Kent. He was educated at Elementary and Simon Langton Grammar Schools, joining the Merchant Navy in 1939. He served with the Merchant Navy until 1942, when he joined the Royal Navy on Special Services, doing duty on evacuations and landings in Italy, North Africa, Burma, Madagascar and the Greek Islands.

After being awarded the Albert Medal, he left the Navy in 1947 with the rate of Acting Chief Petty Officer.

'HM Cable Ship *St Margarets* was lying at Hay Wharf, Malta, on 20th June 1947, when a Chief Petty Officer, entering the No 2 cable tank, was overcome by gas. The First Lieutenant, the Boatswain, and four ratings entered the tank to rescue him and were themselves all overcome.

Leading Seaman May then entered the tank, and, in a series of rescues, secured a line with a timber hitch round each of the seven men, so enabling them to be hauled on deck. He did this by taking deep breaths, and holding them. Speed was essential, and to have waited for apparatus would have been fatal. He made six separate attempts and although the first victim of the gas died later, he was able to save the lives of all those who had followed him.

Philip May, GC, pictured on board his ketch.

94

After his third venture, Leading Seaman May was himself so exhausted by the fumes and exertion that a ship-mate offered to relieve him, but he himself was overcome and required to be rescued. May therefore continued his gallant work single handed until the task was completed. Seven men owe their lives to his selfless bravery and determination.' (LG 25th November 1947)

Philip May had a variety of jobs between 1947 and 1949 and then became an electrical engineer, after studying at night school. He gained a Higher National Certificate in Electrical and Mechanical Engineering after studying at Canterbury Technical College. From 1954, he travelled extensively abroad, mainly in the Middle East and Africa. He retired in 1980 and lives on his own 60-foot ketch.

Mr May is married and has four children. He and his wife, Dee, write in their spare time.

Other medals held by Philip May are: 1939–45 Star, Africa Star, Atlantic Star, Burma Star, Italy Star, War Medal and Silver Jubilee Medal 1977.

His hobby he describes as his boat.

Arthur Richard Cecil BUTSON, GC, OMM, CD, O StJ
(formerly AM)

Arthur Richard Cecil Butson was born in China of British parents on 24th October 1922. He was educated in England at Leighton Park School, Cambridge University and University College Hospital, graduating MB, BChir in 1945.

He served in the Home Guard and a Light Rescue Squad in London during the air raids and as a medical officer with the Falkland Islands Dependencies Survey in the Antarctic from 1946 to 1948. During his year in the Antarctic, the expedition included Kevin Walton, GC (q.v.) and the party found a route for dog teams over the 5,000-foot high mountains of the Antarctic or Grahamland Peninsula and surveyed the last thousand miles of the most inaccessible coastline of the world. For distinguished service in Antarctica, Doctor Butson was awarded the Polar Medal.

Doctor Butson won the Albert Medal for the following act of extreme gallantry:

'On the evening of 26th July 1947, an American member of the Ronne Antarctic Research Expedition fell into the crevasse some six miles from Base. Two teams were sent to the rescue but the hazards of crossing a heavily crevassed glacier were much increased by darkness and it was not until 4 o'clock on the morning of 27th July that the crevasse into which the American had fallen was located. Butson immediately volunteered to be lowered into the crevasse where he found the American tightly wedged 106 feet down and suffering from shock and exhaustion. For nearly an hour he had to chip the ice away in an extremely confined space in order to free the American who was brought to the surface and placed inside a tent. Butson then rendered the necessary medical aid and at dawn a return to Base was made carrying the American on one of the sledges.' (LG 28th September 1948)

The American, Peterson, was active for the remainder of his year in Antarctica, took a second degree at Harvard, served as an officer with the US Marines in Korea and is believed to be alive and well at the time of writing.

95

Butson did post-graduate surgical studies in London until 1952, when he emigrated to Canada, settling in Hamilton, Ontario in 1953, where he has practised as a surgeon ever since. With the establishment of McMaster University Medical School in Hamilton in 1970, he joined the part-time faculty, ending with the appointment of Clinical Professor in the Department of Surgery. He was Chief of Staff of St Joseph's Hospital, a 600-bed teaching hospital, for two years and Head of the Service of General Surgery for many years. He has published about twenty papers on surgical topics.

In 1956, Doctor Butson joined the Canadian Militia as Medical Officer to the Royal Hamilton Light Infantry Regiment. He later transferred to and commanded Hamilton's Militia Medical Company, with the rank of Lieutenant-Colonel. During his command, the unit twice won the trophy for the best militia medical unit in Canada. He later became the Militia Area Surgeon for central Canada. During his militia service, Butson took the Canadian Arctic winter warfare course and qualified as a parachutist at the age of 55! He established a Militia Airborne surgical team. One winter he commanded a Canadian Field Surgical Team on a Norwegian Army Field Hospital exercise. He was President of the Defence Medical Association of Canada and represented Canada medically on the NATO Reserve Officers Association (CIOMR) for four years. For his services to the Canadian Forces, he was appointed Honorary Surgeon to Her Majesty the Queen in 1977 and was made an Officer of the Order of Military Merit of Canada in 1982.

Doctor Butson has been active with St John's Ambulance for many years and is an Officer of the Order of St John.

Mountaineering is one of his hobbies and he has climbed extensively in the Canadian Rockies, Baffin Island, the Antarctic, the Alps and led a climbing expedition to the Hindu

The Rescue Party sets out on 26th July 1947.

96

Dr A. R. C. Butson, GC (left), with Kevin Walton, GC, DSC.

Kush in the Western Himalaya. During his spare time, he raises Galloway beef cattle on his farm near Hamilton, where he lives with his wife.

In addition to the other medals mentioned above, Doctor Butson holds the Defence Medal, the Queen's Silver Jubilee Medal 1977 and the Canadian Forces Decoration. His Albert Medal is now on display at the University College Hospital Medical School.

Eric William Kevin WALTON, GC, DSC (formerly AM)

Kevin Walton was born on 15th May 1918 in Japan, of British missionary parents. He was educated at Monkton Combe School and then studied engineering at Imperial College, London University, at which time he developed an interest in mountaineering.

At the outbreak of war he joined the Royal Navy as an engineer officer. He was on the battleship HMS *Rodney* during the sea battle against the German battleship *Bismarck*. He served mainly in destroyers and won the DSC (LG 27th April 1943) when he was Engineer on the destroyer HMS *Onslow* in 1942, in the naval action off the North Cape of Norway, against the German battleships *Lutzow* and *Hipper*. He played a major part in keeping his badly damaged ship afloat and steaming. Later, in North Altantic convoy duties, he was Mentioned in Despatches as Engineer Officer of HMS *Duncan*. He was also involved in the naval battle of the Malta convoys. At the end of 1945, he sailed for the Antarctic as a member of the Falkland Islands Dependencies Survey and won the Albert Medal in the following circumstances:

'At about 12 noon on 24th August 1946, while on a sledging journey, a member of the Survey fell through a badly-bridged crevasse and disappeared. Major Tonkin had fallen some forty feet and was jammed in a narrow part of the crevasse. Ropes were lowered to him and he managed to get loops round his forearms, but no higher, and it was found impossible to pull him out as he was jammed in the ice. Lieutenant Walton volunteered to be lowered in the crevasse to free Major Tonkin by chipping. As an ice axe could not be used in the constricted space of the crevasse, the spike was sawn off and used as a hand tool. Lieutenant Walton was lowered down a wider part of the crevasse and worked his way along until he reached and succeeded in freeing Major Tonkin, who was eventually pulled to the surface, after having been three hours down the crevasse. During that time Lieutenant Walton was lowered down to him on five separate occasions, remaining down for considerable periods on each occasion. His persistence was most commendable and it was solely due to his efforts that Major Tonkin was finally rescued.' (LG 8th June 1948)

During two years in the Antarctic, Mr Walton played a prominent part in finding a route over the mountainous Antarctic or Grahamland Peninsula and laying the foundation for the accurate survey of one thousand miles of the most inaccessible and previously unmapped coastline of the world. Accompanied by Dr Richard Butson (q.v.) and three others, he climbed several unclimbed peaks in the region of Marguerite Bay in the Antarctic (where, incidentally, he won his AM). For distinguished service in Antarctica, Mr Walton was awarded the Polar Medal.

Kevin Walton has had an unusual and interesting life. He was one of the original instructors in the Outward Bound Mountain School in the Lake District. He has taught workshop engineering at Oundle School, the Royal Naval College, Dartmouth and at Malvern College. He has been involved in 'Windows on Technology' sponsored by several engineering institutes. He is an Associate Member of the Institute of Civil Engineers and is most interested in 'British Voluntary Service Overseas'. He has been involved in the construction of a nuclear power station in Wales. He is the author of *Two Years in the Antarctic*, *A Portrait of Antarctica* and *Great Achievements in Engineering – Making Things Work*.

Kevin Walton and his wife, Ruth, have four children; three daughters and a son. They live in Cornwall, but even after the official retirement age, one doubts that Kevin Walton is often idle!

In addition to the honours mentioned above, Kevin Walton holds the 1939–45 Star, Atlantic Star, Africa Star, War Medal and Silver Jubilee Medal 1977. It is quite characteristic of him that he declined to hand in his AM for exchange, preferring to retain his original award. It appears that he turned up for his investiture of the Albert Medal wearing the wrong ribbon, which was the subject of an exchange of light-hearted words between himself and His Majesty King George VI, himself an expert on medals and ribbons.

Joseph LYNCH, GC, BEM (formerly AM)

Joseph Lynch was born on 6th November 1912 in the Somerville area of Wallasey in Cheshire (now Merseyside). He attended Somerville School, Wallasey.

From 1927 to 1929, he worked firstly as a shop assistant and then as a shop fitter before

Left: Joseph Lynch, GC, BEM, with his wife and daughter at Buckingham Palace.
Right: Joseph Lynch, GC, BEM.

joining the Royal Navy on 29th May 1929. He was married in July 1939 to his wife, Elizabeth, whom he has known since schooldays. They have one son.

Mr Lynch spent over twenty-four years in the Royal Navy, retiring as a Chief Petty Officer on 15th September 1953. He served in the Atlantic and North-West Europe theatres during the Second World War and was awarded the British Empire Medal for rescue work on board HMS *Wallace* in 1942 (LG 13th October 1942)

After retirement from the Navy, Mr Lynch worked for Cadbury's at Wallasey for six months before joining Her Majesty's Customs and Excise as an Executive Officer on 10th May 1954. He retired from this job at the end of 1976.

Characteristically, Mr Lynch has not been idle since his official retirement, since he is a member of the Wallasey Branch of the Royal Naval Association and does welfare work for ex-naval personnel below commissioned rank on the Wallasey side of the river. With his wife, he attends the annual Battle of the Atlantic Service held in May in the Anglican Cathedral in Liverpool and he represents the VC and GC Association. He also attends the Zeebrugge and Walcheren Service which is held on the Wallasey Ferry Boat *Iris* (successor to the immortal *Royal Iris*, which took part in the raid).

In addition to his Albert Medal, which is now housed in the Imperial War Museum, and the British Empire Medal, Mr Lynch has been awarded the 1939–45 Star, Atlantic Star (with France and Germany bar), Defence Medal, War Medal, Coronation Medal 1953 and Jubilee Medal 1977. A few years ago, Mr Lynch's AM was stolen from Wallasey Library, where it had been placed for safe keeping after the exchange. However, a collector into whose hands it eventually came, returned it to Mr Lynch, who then gave it, with Home Office permission, to the Imperial War Museum.

As a matter of interest, having been asked to supply some details of his life and service, Mr

Lynch provided no less than fifty hand-written pages of absolutely fascinating reading but which is, unfortunately, far too long to include here. One might only hope it may be possible to publish it separately, since it is a most interesting document. In this account, the author, like so many of his kind, glosses over his principal award in less than three lines!

Joseph Lynch still lives in Wallasey with his wife. Although he formerly numbered among his hobbies all-round sport, boxing, swimming, football and hockey, these have had to give way in later years to his main interest which is, typically, serving his less fortunate fellow men as Welfare Officer of the Wallasey Branch of the RNA.

He was awarded the Albert Medal for service at sea in the Antarctic, one of a number awarded for this area (*vide* Butson and Walton) and another bronze Albert Medal was awarded in 1876 to Lieutenant Carpenter, RN, (father of Admiral Carpenter, VC) for a rescue in Port Stanley Harbour.

'While HMS *Nigeria* was lying at anchor at Port Stanley, Falkland Islands on the night of 26th February 1948, a rating missed his footing on the Jacob's ladder while disembarking from the motor cutter at the port boom and fell into the sea. It was after dark and the sea was rough and at a temperature of 42° Fahrenheit with the wind blowing a fresh gale.

The rating, Leading Seaman Hughes, managed to retain his hold on the Jacob's ladder but, as he was dressed in heavy oilskins, was unable to pull himself up, nor could he make for the cutter owing to the cold state of the sea and the fear of sinking in his heavy clothes.

CPO Lynch heard the pipe for the life-boat while sitting in his mess. Dressed only in a singlet and trousers he immediately went on deck and, on seeing the situation, made his way out along the boom, down the ladder and into the water alongside Hughes. He persuaded Hughes to let go of the ladder and supported him to the motor cutter. To keep out of the way Lynch then swam back to the ladder to wait until Hughes had been hauled into the boat. When Hughes was safe Lynch swam back to the motor cutter and was himself hauled to safety.' (LG 15th June 1948)

David Charles WESTERN, GC (formerly AM)

David Western was born on 26th April 1937. Nothing is known of his early life but he joined the Royal Navy as a regular, being discharged as a Petty Officer.

Apart from Anthony Farrer (*vide* D. Ashburnham), Mr Western was the youngest male recipient of the Albert Medal, being aged only ten at the time of his award.

'On the afternoon of 27th February 1948, David Charles Western, aged 10, was walking on a frozen lake at Osterley Park with three other boys when the ice gave way and his companions fell through the ice. David Western immediately attempted the rescue of each in turn and in his efforts fell through the ice himself. He succeeded in forcing a channel through the ice till he linked up with one of the boys, who was in difficulties, and they came out together. David Western then returned at once, with a thin rope fastened round his waist, to try to save the lives of the other two boys. Though only a moderate swimmer he swam through the channel in the ice, beat at the unbroken ice with his hands and fists, leaning upon it to make it give way, and though the boys had

David Western, GC, meets HRH The Prince of Wales.

slipped under the ice before he could reach them he dived under the surface to look for one of them until he was practically exhausted and had to be pulled back to the bank. This brave work of attempted rescue was sustained for about twenty-five minutes in icy water, and in forcing his way through the sharp ice David Western received multiple abrasions on body, legs and arms.' (LG 13th August 1948)

He gave his Albert Medal to the Victory Museum, Portsmouth Dockyard. Apart from his GC, which he received on 30th November 1972, he has also been awarded the Queen's Silver Jubilee Medal 1977, the Naval Long Service and Good Conduct Medal and Royal Humane Society's Bronze Medal.

He is married and lives in Plymouth.

Kenneth FARROW, GC (formerly AM)

Kenneth Farrow was born on 29th May 1924, a native of County Durham. He was educated at Sedgefield Junior School, County Durham and St Michael's School, Buckingham Palace Road, London. Mr Farrow was employed as a shop assistant from 1938 to 1943, when he joined the Royal Air Force and served with 218 Squadron in Suffolk as an Air Gunner, attaining the rank of Flight Sergeant and being awarded the Defence Medal and War Medal for his war service.

On 7th February 1947, he joined the Cardiff City Police, later the South Wales Constabulary, retiring on 10th September 1972 as a Sergeant (Road Safety Officer). After retirement

101

PC Kenneth Farrow, AM, in 1948 at Buckingham Palace.

from the police, he joined the Traffic Management Section of Glamorgan County Council.

Mr Farrow married his wife, Joan, a Cardiff girl, while serving in the RAF and they have a son. The award of the Albert Medal to Kenneth Farrow was made for the following act of gallantry:

'On 21st June 1948, Constable Kenneth Farrow of the Cardiff City Police Force attempted to rescue a 4-year-old boy from drowning in the Feeder, Pembroke Terrace, Cardiff.

The incident occurred at about 7 pm when Constable Farrow was on police patrol duty. He saw a number of persons running, and, on enquiry, was informed that a child had fallen into the Feeder. He at once ran to the place, divested himself of his police clothing, dived into the Feeder and swam underneath a long concrete covering for a distance of about 180 yards in search of the child.

The Feeder is an aqueduct running under concrete slabs and supplying water from the River Taff to Cardiff Docks. It was uncovered at the spot where the child fell in. The speed of the current was about six miles an hour and, whereas headroom at the end of the concrete covering is 2 feet 2 inches (where the accident occurred) it decreases till it is only 6 inches. The water is black with a considerable amount of mud or silt at the bottom, and it is not possible to stand up in the water with head above water level.

Although the child's body was not recovered till later, Constable Farrow greatly exhausted himself in the search and in the ordeal of making his way back against the current, with very little facility for obtaining a proper handgrip. According to witnesses, he was in the waters of the Feeder and underneath the concrete slabs for about a quarter of an hour, in pitch darkness.

Constable Farrow joined the Cardiff City Police on 7th February 1947. He was then a poor swimmer, but he obtained his Life Saving certificate and medallion a few months later. He is not yet a strong swimmer, but unhesitatingly risked his life under conditions which would have daunted even the strongest swimmer.

Constable Farrow's gallantry was commended by the Coroner and highly praised by the witnesses of his action.' (LG 15th October 1948)

Kenneth Farrow, GC.

He also received the Gold and Silver Medals of the Welsh ASA and the Carnegie Hero Fund Trust Certificate. He was invested with the GC on 30th November 1972 and presented his Albert Medal to the National Museum of Wales at Cardiff. In addition to those awards mentioned, Mr Farrow holds the Police Exemplary Service Medal and the Queen's Silver Jubilee Medal 1977. He lives in Glamorganshire and enjoys fishing and gardening.

Alfred Raymond LOWE, GC (formerly AM)

Alfred Raymond Lowe was born in London on 14th June 1931, and educated at Watts Naval Training School from 1943 to 1947. He entered the Royal Navy as a Boy in January 1947, on a scholarship.

He was not sixteen when he won the Albert Medal as a Boy First Class for a very brave rescue during a disaster when many lives were lost.

'At 2245 hours on 17th October 1948 a liberty boat returning from Weymouth Pier to HMS *Illustrious* in Portland Harbour overturned and sank 50 to 100 yards from the ship's stern, with fifty-one men on board. Boy Lowe was trapped under the canopy, struggled free and surfaced. He saw a life-belt a short distance from him which had been thrown from HMS *Illustrious* and swam to it. He then removed his overcoat and shoes and swam towards the ship. When he was under the stern a line was thrown to him. At this moment he heard a faint cry of "Help" and on looking round saw that a Midshipman who was about ten yards away, was in great difficulty.

He grabbed the line and swam to the Midshipman who was unconscious by the time he reached him. He endeavoured to turn him over to keep his head above water but found this impossible and still holding him was pulled to the ship's side. A fog buoy was then lowered and he managed to drag the Midshipman on to this and to hold on to him until a Petty Officer came down the rope to assist him. Together they secured the

Midshipman who was then hoisted on board. The accident took place in eight fathoms of water, in a rough sea with a strong wind blowing.

Although the Midshipman subsequently died, Boy Lowe acted with complete disregard for his own life in leaving his place of safety in an attempt to save him. His action in endangering his own life in this accident in which twenty-nine men lost their lives was in accordance with the highest traditions of the Royal Navy.' (LG 8th February 1949)

Alfred Lowe later qualified as a radar operator and shallow-water diver and served as a diver on board HMS *Concord* during the Korean War. He was Mentioned in Despatches (LG 3rd October 1952) 'for distinguished service in operations in Korean waters'.

Mr Lowe was married in October 1959 to Hilda May Denham and they have three

A. R. Lowe, GC, in 1974.

daughters. They live in Auckland, New Zealand, where Mr Lowe had emigrated in 1963. He is presently a representative for a marine boatbuilding company.

The Albert Medal was presented by King George VI at an investiture at Buckingham Palace in March 1949 and he received the George Cross from the Governor-General of New Zealand at Government House, New Zealand, on 12th April 1973. Other medals held by Mr Lowe are: Korea Medal, United Nations Korea Medal and Queen's Silver Jubilee Medal 1977. He resigned from the Royal Navy in July 1959 as a Petty Officer.

Margaret VAUGHAN, GC (formerly AM)

Margaret Vaughan was born in Cardiff on 25th November 1934, the daughter of Sergeant (later Superintendent) James Vaughan of Cardiff City Police. She was educated at Penarth County Grammar School for Girls and trained as a State Registered Nurse at Oldchurch Hospital, Romford, Essex, where she qualified in 1956. She then trained as a midwife in London and Cardiff and qualified as State Certified Midwife in 1957.

Commissioned into the Queen Alexandra's Royal Army Nursing Corps (QARANC) as a Lieutenant in 1957, she served in the UK, Mauritius, Nairobi and Hanover, Germany, before resigning on marriage in 1961, when she married Captain John Purves, REME, at Llandaff Cathedral on 20th May 1961. They have three children; two girls and a boy.

Mrs Purves was the last living person to be awarded the Albert Medal; subsequent awards were posthumous until all awards ceased on 21st November 1971. She is also the youngest surviving lady holder of the GC.

Margaret Vaughan, AM, with her father.

'On 28th May 1949, a party of Scouts aged between 11 and 15 years, visiting Sully Island were cut off by the rising tide from the causeway which led to the mainland. Most of the boys got safely across, but two of them were forced off the causeway by the strong tide. The leader of the party returned to help the elder boy but in the struggle he too became exhausted. Margaret Vaughan (aged 14 years) saw from the beach the difficulties they were in. She undressed and swam towards them over a distance of some 30 yards in cold, rough water and against strong currents due to the rising tide. On reaching them she towed the boy to the shore while he supported himself by grasping the straps of her costume and his leader's coat. At about ten feet from the shore a life belt was thrown in which the boy was placed by the other two and the three reached the shore safely. Margaret Vaughan's action probably saved the life of the Scout leader as well as that of the elder boy.

Meanwhile, John Howard Davies (aged 13 years) had safely reached the mainland when he saw that his friend, who was unable to swim, was being forced away from the causeway into deep water. He stripped to the waist and went back along the causeway to help him. By swimming out he was able to grasp his friend and hold him up in the water. Both boys shouted for help and it was obvious that they would not get ashore unaided. By this time a rescue boat had put out from the shore but Davies became exhausted by his efforts and before the boat could reach them he was forced to release his hold on his friend and they drifted apart. The boat rescued the friend but no further sign of Davies was seen. He body was subsequently recovered. There is no doubt that in returning to the aid of his friend after he himself had reached safety Davies gave his life in this rescue attempt.' (LG 1st November 1949)

105

John Howard Davies was posthumously awarded a well-deserved Albert Medal for this incident.

Margaret Vaughan was fêted when the news of her exploit leaked out. As well as the Albert Medal, she was also awarded the Royal Humane Society's Certificate on Vellum and the Certificate of the Carnegie Hero Fund Trust, in 1949. She was invested with her Albert Medal by King George VI in March 1950.

Since exchanging her Albert Medal for the George Cross, Mrs Purves has been a keen and active member of the VC and GC Association and has been a Committee Member since 1972. She is particularly interested in the welfare of members. Together with the late Commander D. H. Evans, GC, she attended the Investiture of HRH the Prince of Wales at Caernarfon in 1969, representing the VC and GC Association.

In addition to her GC, Mrs Purves also holds the Coronation Medal 1953 and the Jubilee Medal 1977. She attended the Queen's Silver Jubilee Review of the British Army of the Rhine at Sennelager in 1977.

Mrs Purves now lives in Wiltshire and she presented her AM for display to the National Museum of Wales.

Mrs Margaret Purves, GC.

THE EDWARD MEDAL

The pedigree of the Edward Medal is of much more recent origin than that of the Albert Medal, the Royal Warrant which brought the EM into existence being dated 13th July 1907. This created an award for saving life in mines, consisted of two classes, First and Second Class, and was awarded to 'those who, in saving or endeavouring to save the lives of others . . . have endangered their own lives'.

It became apparent in a very short time that the scope of the Edward Medal required enlarging and consequently, on 1st December 1909, a second variety of medal was introduced for saving life, or endeavouring to save life, in industry generally. This, too, consisted of medals of the First and Second Class and the ribbon for all medals was identical; dark blue with gold stripes at each edge, $1\frac{1}{2}$ inches in width.

Two reverses were used for the Edward Medal for industry, the first being current in 1910–11 and the second from 1912 to 1971 (see illustrations overleaf).

On 28th August 1917, a Royal Warrant changed the titles of the Edward Medal to 'Edward Medal in Silver' and 'Edward Medal', the latter being in Bronze. At about this time, also, recipients were permitted to use the post-nominal initials 'EM'.

In 1971, a Royal Warrant dated 15th December, effective 21st October 1971 (*vide* the Albert Medal) was issued, revoking the Edward Medal and giving surviving recipients on that date (21st October) the option of exchanging the medal for the George Cross. As with the Albert Medal, not all chose to do so and nine of the sixty-eight eligible retained their original awards, of whom two were holders of the EM in Silver. One is still alive at the time of writing, Harry Robinson (q.v.). The other was the late Arthur Devere Thomas.

Unlike the Albert Medal, bars were authorised for the Edward Medal, although only two were awarded, both to Silver medals, in 1910 and 1911. Neither recipient survived to exchange his medal but it is interesting to speculate, had they done so, whether or not they would both have received the George Cross and bar. There is no reason to suppose that this would not have been so.

The numbers of Edward Medals awarded are as follows:

Silver	—	Mines	—	77	= 102
		Industry	—	25	
Bronze	—	Mines	—	318	= 482
		Industry	—	164	

= 584

Of the above, nine medals went to members of the army (one Silver, eight Bronze – all during the First World War), two members of whom, both Bronze medallists, survived to exchange their awards. Only two, both Bronze medals, were awarded to ladies, neither of whom survived to exchange the medal. The last one (Hannah Hugill) died in 1969.

The Edward Medal is probably the rarest British gallantry award to women and, like the Albert Medal but unlike most other decorations, including the GC, which replaced it, it is not awarded with the ribbon in the shape of a bow.

The earliest incident for which an Edward Medal was exchanged for the George Cross was that involving Percy Roberts Havercroft (q.v.) in 1915 and the last awards of the EM to living recipients were those to Frank Bradley (also the last Silver award to a living recipient), Oswald George Simmonds and Thomas George Manwaring (q.v.), of whom the last named was the only one to exchange his medal (LG 21st June 1949).

Two Silver medal holders are still alive at the end of 1985, out of only nine alive at the time of the exchanges. One is Harry Robinson, mentioned above and the other is Ernest Allport (q.v.).

The highest number of Edward Medals awarded for a single incident was announced in *The London Gazette* of 22nd July 1910. There were two Silver and no fewer than *sixty-three* Bronze medals awarded.

At the time of writing, there are still three men known to be wearing their original EM insignia; one Silver and two Bronze.

The Edward Medal (Mines) reverse.

The Edward Medal (Industry) reverse.

The Edward Medal (Industry) reverse,
second type.

Percy Roberts HAVERCROFT, GC (formerly EM)

Percy Roberts Havercroft was born in Sheffield in 1884 but nothing is known of his early life and schooling.

He spent fifty-one years in the mines and won the Edward Medal in 1915 as a joiner and shaftsman.

Percy Havercroft, GC.

'On the 27th August, 1915, a descending cage containing ten men, collided about half-way down one of the shafts of the Waleswood Colliery, near Sheffield, with an empty ascending cage. The impact was extremely violent, severely injuring all the men and breaking the winding ropes. Both cages were, however, wedged together in the shaft, so that, fortunately, neither of them fell to the bottom, though there was serious danger that they might do so at any moment. A hoppit manned by Tomlinson, Havercroft and Walker was at once sent down to effect the rescue of the imprisoned men. All the men were carried from the damaged car along a girder to the hoppit, which made five descents altogether, the rescue occupying about two hours. During the whole of this time Tomlinson, Havercroft and Walker were exposed to great danger either from the hoppit being upset by the winding ropes swinging in the shaft, or from the damaged cage breaking loose and falling down the shaft.

Wingfield, who was one of the occupants of the descending cage, had both legs fractured, and received a severe wound on the thigh and a wound on the head. He seized hold of another man who had fallen half-way through the bottom of the cage, and held him up until he was rescued. During the whole time he displayed the greatest coolness and bravery, despite his very severe injuries, and insisted on all his fellow workmen being removed to a place of safety before allowing himself to be taken to the surface.'
(LG 22nd June 1917)

Albert Henry Tomlinson, John Walker and Edward Wingfield were all awarded the Edward Medal for this incident. Mr Havercroft died in Sheffield on 15th July 1976.

Arthur Frederick EDWARDS, GC (formerly EM)
Charles Thomas HARRIS, GC (formerly EM)

Owing to censorship restrictions, no fully detailed citation appeared in *The London Gazette* in respect of the above two men, who were both soldiers at the time, and were awarded the Edward Medal in company with three others in April 1916. Only the following bare facts appeared in *The London Gazette* of the time:

A fine portrait of Arthur Frederick Edwards, GC, about the time of his award.

'On account of their gallant conduct in assisting in the rescue work on the occasion of the explosion which occurred at Faversham on 2nd April 1916.' (LG 22nd January 1918)

It will be seen that a delay of almost two years elapsed between the action for which the medals were awarded and the gazetting of them. This was due to various bureaucratic machinations which had gone on in the interim in an effort to win military personnel involved in rescue work the same recognition as that bestowed upon civilians in like circumstances, although a solitary private soldier, one William James Wiltshire, *had* been decorated along with the seven civilians.

Such, even then, was the intricacy of awarding suitable bravery medals, that all the military personnel involved, numbering some seventeen, had already received the Meritorious Service Medal which, curiously, was not subsequently cancelled upon the award of the Edward Medals to the four concerned (the fifth was an officer and not, therefore, eligible for the MSM). Since the award of the EM to Private Wiltshire was, so to speak, a 'direct' award, he did not, of course, receive the MSM.

The following soldiers were awarded the Edward Medal, in addition to those named above: Bombardier Bert Dugdale, RFA, Corporal Charles Ashley, RFA and Lieutenant John Morley Stebbings, RFA. The latter subsequently became a Lieutenant-Colonel with the MC and ED and his death was reported at Ramsgate on 2nd November 1966.

Arthur Frederick Edwards was born on 28th May 1895, the only son of Mr and Mrs J. F. Edwards of Messrs J. and J. Edwards, Outfitters, Tavern Street, Ipswich, Suffolk and Lowestoft. He was educated at Ipswich Grammar and Bishop's Stortford Schools and before the First World War, he worked for eighteen months with his father and after this with Ogdens Ltd, Outfitters of Rochester, Kent.

He was married to Edna Mary (née Sanders) and they had two sons, one of whom is deceased.

Mr Edwards served in the First World War in the Royal Garrison Artillery, attaining the rank of Bombardier. He received the British War Medal, Victory Medal, Queen's Silver Jubilee Medal and Meritorious Service Medal, being invested with the Edward Medal on 17th July 1919, which he presented to the Ipswich Museum when he exchanged it for the George Cross.

Mr Edwards died on 28th May 1984, aged 89.

Not much is known of Charles Thomas Harris; his date and place of birth and details of his early life and schooling are a mystery.

He was one of five servicemen to win the Edward Medal for courage at the Faversham explosion, as outlined above, and although he was alive at the time of the exchanges, he elected to retain his original award.

He was a member of the Royal Engineers at the time, serving with 1st/4th Company, Kent (Fortress) RE and like A. F. Edwards, he also received the MSM. He was awarded the Territorial Force Efficiency Medal in 1920, his then service number being 540069 and received a bar to this award in 1931, when his service number was 2201492. His EM and MSM are now in the Museum of the Royal Engineers at Chatham.

Mr Harris died at Gillingham, Kent, on 28th January 1972.

Archibald YOUNG, GC (formerly EM)

Archibald Young, GC.

29th February 1892 and educated at Castle Douglas School and Dumfries Academy. He qualified as a Chartered Accountant in 1915 and was thereafter employed as such. He was married and had one daughter.

In 1917, Mr Young enlisted into the King's Own Scottish Borderers but was released after a few weeks to go and work at Roslin, near Edinburgh, and here it was that he won his Edward Medal.

'On the 20th June 1916, a small explosion occurred at 10 am in a building at the Roslin Explosives Factory. Morrison and Sang, who were aware that four girls were in the building, which had caught fire, and that the building was full of explosives, at once ran towards it. As they approached two of the girls came out and fell unconscious on the grass. The building was now blazing furiously; but Morrison and Sang, who knew the position of the explosives within, used the fire buckets so as to allay the flames in the dangerous quarter, and to enable Morrison to dash in. He groped through the smoke, which was dense white, found one girl and passed her out to Young, who had arrived meanwhile; he then returned for the second girl, and eventually brought her out, while Young placed the first girl on a bogey, which he thrust along the line out of danger, and then returned for the second. Sang meanwhile kept the fire down as far as possible with water buckets.

During the whole of this time small explosions were continually taking place within the building, and immediately after the second rescue a heavy explosion occurred, which flattened down part of it. Twelve minutes after the original explosion the whole building blew up.' (LG 1st January 1917)

William Alexander Morrison was awarded the Edward Medal of the First Class (in Silver) and George Sang the Edward Medal of the Second Class (in Bronze) for this incident.

Mr Young also received the Certificate of the Carnegie Hero Fund Trust.

He enjoyed gardening in his spare time. At the time of the exchanges, Mr Young was the senior surviving holder of the Edward Medal, in terms of date of award.

He died on 7th November 1976, aged 84.

John McCABE, GC (formerly EM)

John McCabe was born on 6th December 1901 in Scotland and went to school at St Mary's, Longriggend, near Airdrie. He was a miner from the age of 16 until he retired at 65. He won the Edward Medal, when only 17 years of age for an act of great courage in 1918, at Stanrigg Colliery, Airdrie.

John McCabe, GC, with his family.

'On the 9th July 1918, there was an inrush of moss into the workings. McCabe, with two other drawers and three miners, was at the bottom of number 3 shaft when they were told that the moss had broken in. The two other boys and the three men at once ascended the shaft and escaped. McCabe however, knowing that there were men at the face who might be cut off, returned for a quarter of a mile and warned the men. He and the men he had warned were ultimately collected and raised by another shaft. When he returned to the face, McCabe did not know where the break had occurred, or whether the moss might not at any moment fill the workings through which he returned, as in fact it soon afterwards did. He faced a grave and unknown danger, which might have been fatal, in order to enable others to escape.' (LG 13th June 1919)

Mr McCabe also received a silver pocket watch from the Carnegie Hero Fund Trust.

He was married and he and his wife, Annie (née Dowdalls), had a son and a daughter. His hobbies were football and horse racing.

He died at Caldercruix, Lanarkshire, on 29th January 1974.

Thomas Atkinson WHITEHEAD, GC (formerly EM)

Thomas Atkinson Whitehead was born in County Tipperary, Ireland, on 17th July 1887 and attended local schools.

He went to England and while working for Messrs Brotherton & Co Ltd, Sunderland, won the Edward Medal for a gallant but vain rescue attempt in a tar distillery.

'The stills used at the works are large cylinders ten feet in diameter and twenty feet deep. While one of these stills was standing empty, and, as it was thought, disconnected from the adjoining stills, a workman named Dougherty descended it by means of a rope ladder through the small manhole, fifteen inches in diameter, in the cover. When he reached the bottom he collapsed. His mate realising that gas must have accumulated in the still, immediately shouted for help and ran to get a rope. A workman named George Rogers, who was working near, without waiting for a rope, immediately went down the still for the purpose of rescuing Dougherty, but he was also overcome. Other workmen had arrived in the meantime, and one of them, William

Thomas Whitehead, GC (seated) with members of his family.

King, at once entered the still with a handkerchief round his mouth and a rope attached to his body. He was overcome and had to be pulled out. Thereupon Whitehead made two attempts to reach the men at the bottom of the still, first equipped with a gauze respirator and then with a hood with oxygen pumped into it, but on both occasions he had to be pulled out. King then made a further attempt at rescue, and went in wearing a respirator and having a safety-belt round his body. By this time other workmen had removed the pitch-pipe from the bottom of the still and began to force air in, and in the second attempt King was successful in reaching the men who had been overcome. He attached ropes to the bodies and they were drawn out; artificial respiration was tried but they were found to be dead.

The danger due to sulphuretted hydrogen accumulating in the still was well known in the works, and King and Whitehead were fully aware of the risks they ran; they acted promptly and courageously and showed coolness and intelligence in the measures taken for the attempted rescue of their fellow-workmen.' (LG 5th September 1922)

William King was also awarded the Edward Medal for his part in this incident.

Mr Whitehead qualified as an engineer before returning to his native Ireland. He was married with one daughter.

Thomas Whitehead declined to exchange his Edward Medal for the George Cross and he died in Ireland on 27th August 1973, aged 85.

Bert CRAIG, GC (formerly EM in Silver)

Bert Craig at Buckingham Palace showing his EM to his Member of Parliament, The Hon George Hall, MP for Aberdare.

A good studio portrait of Bert Craig, EM, showing him wearing his medal.

Bert Craig was born on 11th March 1899 in Bristol and educated at Duffryn Boys' School, Mountain Ash, Glamorgan. He became a coal miner, an occupation he followed all his working life, apart from war service in the First World War.

He won his Edward Medal in 1922 in the following circumstances:

'On 14th November 1922, in the course of operations at Nixon's Navigation Colliery at Mountain Ash, Glamorganshire, a workman named Jones was completely buried by a heavy fall of stones and rubbish. Four other men were present at the time, and made some attempt to get Jones out, as although they could not see him, they could hear him moaning. Further falls, however, took place, and the four men, considering the risk too great, retreated under cover.

At this moment Bert Craig, another workman at the Colliery, arrived on the scene, and hearing of what had happened at once ran to where Jones was buried and began to remove the stones. In spite of his appeals for help, the other men hung back until the falls ceased, but they then came to Craig's assistance, and Jones was extricated. All the time falls were taking place, and within two minutes of Jones being pulled out so large a fall took place that both he and Craig would certainly have been killed.

Craig's action was a very gallant one, and he undoubtedly saved Jones's life. He was working under conditions of very great danger, and his conduct appears even more

Bert Craig, GC, about 1965.

gallant in view of the fact that he suffers from the result of a severe bullet wound in the head, and any blow might have been fatal.' (LG 1st June 1923)

Bert Craig also received the Carnegie Hero Fund Trust Certificate for this brave rescue. In July 1972, he exchanged his Edward Medal for the George Cross and the former is now in Cardiff Museum. Mr Craig was married but he and his wife, Millicent, had no children.

By 1931, Mr Craig had qualified as a Swedish masseur, an art he practised for the rest of his life in his spare time. He was also interested in the St John's Ambulance and was a Serving Brother of the Order of St John. For his First World War service, he held the 1914 Star, British War and Victory Medals, and he was awarded the Queen's Silver Jubilee Medal in 1977. He died on 14th December 1978, aged 79.

Alfred Ernest MORRIS, GC (formerly EM)

Alfred Ernest Morris was born on 19th August 1881 and educated at Norwich Grammar School. He was one of thirteen children; seven boys and six girls. On leaving school, he had an amazing variety of jobs, including: service in the army (Life Guards and Scots Guards), musician with the London Symphony and Cape Town Orchestras, conductor, hotelier, shop-keeper, farmer, pioneer, contractor, builder, actor, singer and miner. In between times, he managed to find time to do courses in engineering and building management!

It was while working as a miner that he won the Edward Medal in 1923 in the following circumstances:

'On May 29th 1923, at Obuasi, Ashanti, while a cyanide solution was being prepared in a vat on the premises of the Ashanti Goldfields Corporation, a native, named Robert, who was working in the vat contrary to orders was overcome by the fumes. Two other natives Sikeyena and Guruba attempted to rescue him but were themselves overcome. Mr Chardin, who was on the spot realised the danger and the need for immediate action if the men were to be saved. Without hesitation he entered the vat by a ladder but was himself overpowered by the fumes. Mr Morris, and Mr Skinner, the shift engineer, arrived and between them managed to drag Mr Chardin out of the vat. Skinner then collapsed but Morris tied a rope round himself, re-entered the vat and eventually succeeded in bringing out the three natives alive. Unfortunately Mr Chardin and the two natives Sikeyena and Robert succumbed, but the conduct of Mr Chardin and Mr Morris was extremely gallant and Mr Morris undoubtedly risked his life in entering the vat no less than three times in his work of rescue.' (LG 4th July 1924)

Alfred Ernest Morris as a young soldier in the Life Guards. Inset: Capt A. E. Morris, GC.

The investiture of the Edward Medal took place in December 1924.

Alfred Morris married twice and had four daughters. He served in three wars – the Boer War, and the First and Second World Wars – a remarkable record. For his services, he was awarded the Queen's South Africa Medal with clasps for 'Wittebergen', 'Transvaal' and 'Cape Colony', the King's South Africa Medal, 1939–45 Star, Africa Star and War Medal. Strangely, although he served in East Africa with the African Pioneer Corps combat unit in Kenya and the Rhodesia Mounted Rifles in Umtali during the First World War, he appears to have received no official recognition of his service by way of medals.

He was serving in the Life Guards in 1910 and led the funeral procession of King Edward VII on the Drum Horse. His picture was used in *The History of The Household Cavalry*, Volume 2, as well as King Edward's memoirs.

On demobilisation in 1945, Alfred Morris retired as a Major but he was permitted to retain the rank of Captain. He was the oldest man (91) to exchange his Edward Medal for the George Cross, which he did at the Embassy in Gabarone in December 1972, presenting his EM to the British Museum.

Captain Morris' hobbies were as varied as his jobs and included writing, travel, music, public speaking, hunting and African Languages. He was also a keen Freemason.

He died in Bulawayo, after a short illness, on 24th November 1973, aged 94.

Harry WILSON, GC (formerly EM)

Harry Wilson was born on 13th January 1903 and went to school at Smallthorne, Packmoor and Mow Cop, all in Stoke-on-Trent. From school, aged about 12, he went straight into the coal mines, working at Harrisea Colliery, then at Dinnington, Yorkshire, during the General Strike.

He won the Edward Medal in March 1924 for the following act of gallantry.

'An inrush of water took place on 10th March 1924, at the Harriseahead Colliery in Staffordshire. Most of the workmen had already left the mine but one man named Booth, who had been working alone about 130 yards from the bottom of the shaft, was missing. Mr Baker, the manager, was told that it was impossible to rescue him. The bottom of the pit was three parts full of water which was still rising.

Baker called for volunteers. Wilson was one of five men who responded and descended into the mine by a foot-rail. The rescue party reached a ventilation door which they dared not open owing to the pressure of water behind it and they therefore prepared to retire. Baker, who had followed, insisted that Booth could not be left. Wilson alone volunteered to continue, and with Baker forced the ventilation door, allowing the water to escape gradually. They they waded to Booth, reaching him after great difficulty, and all three men were eventually drawn to the surface.

Both Baker and Wilson ran a very great risk of being trapped. They could not tell to what height the water would rise and had it reached the roof all would have lost their lives.' (LG 22nd August and 2nd September 1924)

Paling Baker was also awarded the Edward Medal for this rescue.

Harry Wilson received the Order of Industrial Heroism for this act and the Carnegie Hero Fund Trust subscribed towards his training as a Deputy. He was invested with the Edward

Above: Harry Wilson, GC, with his wife and family. Inset: Harry Wilson, EM, at about the time of his award, 1925.

Medal on 12th February 1925.

Mr Wilson was married with two daughters and he and his wife Mary celebrated their golden wedding anniversary in July 1975. She died in 1984.

A man of many talents, Mr Wilson served in the St John's Ambulance Brigade for twenty-five years and was a keen amateur musician and woodworker. He played the violin in the Scholar Green Orchestra for many years.

Just before the Second World War, he went to work for the local council at Kidsgrove, Worcestershire, staying with them for thirty years and retiring in 1968. He then spent four years as a night watchman at Billingtons and Newtons in Hanley, Staffordshire.

Mr Wilson died at Stoke-on-Trent, Staffordshire, on 26th March 1986, aged 83, having received the Queen's Silver Jubilee Medal in 1977.

Robert PEARSON, GC (formerly EM)

Robert Pearson was born in Stockport, Cheshire, on 4th July 1896 and went to Hollywood Park School. His mother died when he was 2 and his father when he was 10. Until he won the Edward Medal, in 1925, he was a keen sportsman, being interested in football, boxing and athletics. He worked for thirty-five years as a dyer and bleacher for Henry Marsland Ltd, retiring in 1955. During this time he also acted as caretaker for Central Hall, Lower Hillgate, Stockport.

'On the 11th July 1925, while two boys named Stothert and Bowden were working in a vat at the works of Messrs H. Marsland Ltd, at Stockport, there was a sudden inrush of scalding liquid and steam owing to a mistake made in opening the pipe of another vat. The screams of the scalded boys attracted the attention of other workers and attempts were made to extricate them through the manholes. Bowden was successfully drawn out but Stothert after reaching the manhole fell back into the vat owing to the burnt flesh of his hand giving way. Pearson, a

Robert Pearson, GC, his first medal *The Daily Herald* Order of Industrial Heroism.

labourer employed at the works, then came upon the scene. He saw Bowden pulled out terribly scalded and on hearing that Stothert was still in the vat he at once ran to it. He jumped down the manhole and after groping about found Stothert with some difficulty and hoisted him sufficiently to enable those outside to drag him to the surface. Pearson's feet were severely scalded during his efforts and he was practically unconscious on being drawn to the top.

Both boys succumbed to their injuries but Pearson's effort to save Stothert's life was a very gallant one. Though the steam had been turned off when Pearson entered the vat he was unaware of this and so far as he could tell the vat might have been full of boiling liquid. He had never been inside one of these vats before: all he knew was that he had seen one boy terribly scalded and that there was another boy inside and he faced the risk of attempting the rescue without any regard to his own safety, while neither the scalding he experienced nor the intense pain which he suffered deterred him from persisting in his efforts to get the lad out.' (LG 20th October 1925)

For this act of gallantry, Mr Pearson also received the rare Order of Industrial Heroism from *The Daily Herald* newspaper.

After his rescue attempt, he became a well-known local football trainer and masseur and other interests included bowls and voluntary work for local clubs for the elderly.

He served in the First World War, attaining the rank of Corporal and was awarded the British War and Victory Medals. He had one son. Mr Pearson gave his Edward Medal to the Vernon Park Museum in Stockport and he died on 17th March 1973, aged 76.

Donald FLETCHER, GC (formerly EM)

Donald Fletcher was born on 17th January 1902 in Sheffield and was educated in Sheffield, Worksop and Firbeck. Unusually amongst the miners featured in these pages, mining was only one of the jobs he did during his working life.

He began in 1915 as a grocer's apprentice but went into farming in 1917. He stayed there until 1922, when he became a miner and it was during this period that he won the Edward Medal.

Donald Fletcher, EM, pictured in a contemporary report in the *Worksop Guardian*.

'On the 10th September 1925, a heavy fall of roof to a depth of sixteen feet took place at the Cresswell Colliery in Derbyshire completely burying a miner named Cooper. Some of the larger pieces of the roof became interlocked affording him some protection from the full weight of the fall and thus prevented his being crushed to death. Efforts were made to discover where Cooper lay and it was found that his head was near the edge of the fall so that it was possible to free it from debris. His shoulders were next freed but his body and legs were held fast. The only way in which Cooper could be extricated was that someone should crawl under the debris and by working a passage alongside and over Cooper release him very gradually and stone by stone. Fletcher at once volunteered for this task and was successful after two hours' continuous work. Great patience and skill were required, and in the course of the work Fletcher's body was completely under the fall with his head close to Cooper's feet. Throughout the operation Fletcher was exposed to the risk of being crushed to death either by a second fall or by a settling down of the first fall, and he performed his task skilfully without regarding his own safety. Fletcher's action was a very brave one involving great risk to his own life and, indeed, in the latter stages of the work his position was more dangerous than Cooper's.' (LG 26th January 1926)

Leaving mining in 1935, he became an insurance agent and assistant manager until 1948.

Donald Fletcher, GC, with his family at his reinvestiture.

After that, and finally, he was a civil servant, working for the Department of Health and Social Security until 1968.

Mr Fletcher is married and he and his wife, Mildred, have one son, born on 3rd November 1939. He never served in the Forces but holds the Queen's Silver Jubilee Medal 1977 and his hobbies are gardening and motoring. His Edward Medal is now in the Derby Museum and Art Gallery.

Donald Fletcher lives quietly in retirement in Derbyshire.

George LOCKE, GC (formerly EM)

George Locke was born about 1892 but nothing is known of his early life and schooling.

It was as a Leading Hand with Messrs Dorman Long and Co that he won the Edward Medal for an amazing act of agility and bravery in 1925.

'On the 8th October, 1925, Locke was engaged in the erection of steel work for the rebuilding of the premises of Messrs Bourne & Hollingsworth in Oxford Street. He and another workman named Frederick Dowser were standing on parallel girders on the fourth floor level when Dowser tripped and fell, striking his head in his fall and lying stunned on the girder. The girders on which the men were working were only seven inches in width and were no less than seven feet apart. Locke, on seeing his comrade fall, with great presence of mind immediately leapt across the intervening space and throwing himself upon the legs of the fallen man pinned him to the girder until help arrived and they were dragged back to safety. But for Locke's prompt action there is little doubt that Dowser would have fallen to the ground and been killed. Locke's action was a very brave one and he showed total disregard of his own safety. To spring from one girder to the other at a great height was no small feat and he must have recognised in holding down his comrade that any struggle on the latter's part must endanger the lives of both.' (LG 2nd March 1926)

George Locke also received the Bronze Medallion of the Carnegie Hero Fund Trust for this brave act.

About 1973, Mr Locke was discovered living in an Old People's Home in Dovercourt, Essex. He had no idea he could exchange his Edward Medal for the George Cross and was only persuaded to do so if the Queen herself presented it to him personally.

Sadly, he died on 10th June 1974, just a month before his investiture with the GC, which he received posthumously. He was 82.

George Locke, GC.

James JOHNSTON, GC (formerly EM)

James Johnston was born in Greenock, Scotland, on 12th December 1881. He went to India when he was 4 years old and was educated at St James School, Calcutta. All his working life was spent coal mining with the Government of India, State Railways Coal Department at mines in Central India and the provinces of Bihar and Orissa. He was awarded the Edward Medal for a gallant rescue in India in January 1925.

'On the 7th January 1925 a very heavy fall of roof took place in the Mohpani Colliery of the GIP Railway in India, killing one miner instantaneously and completely burying another named Nanoo Maora. On a report of the accident reaching Mr Kipling, the under-manager of the mine, he went with Mr Johnston, the senior European

James Johnston, GC.

122

overseer, and Nani Khan, a native timber-drawer, and crawling through the fall of stone and earth, eventually got the man out.

Within 20 minutes of their extricating Nanoo, twenty tons of rock fell on the very spot where he had been lying.' (LG 19th March 1926)

James Kipling and Nani Khan were awarded the Edward Medal for their part in this rescue.

James Johnston was an excellent shot and won several trophies for shooting whilst serving with the Auxiliary Force India during and after the First World War. As well as shooting, he was interested in carpentry and reading.

Mr Johnston and his wife returned to the United Kingdom to live in Salisbury, Wiltshire, in September 1948 and they celebrated their diamond wedding anniversary on 28th December 1972. He died in Salisbury on 7th September 1974, aged 93 and his wife on 6th February 1981. They had six children; three boys and three girls. The eldest boy died of diphtheria in India and his second son died as a prisoner of war in Siam (now Thailand) while serving with the Royal Artillery.

William LLOYD, GC (formerly EM)

William Lloyd was born in 1906 but nothing is known of his early life and schooling.

He won the Edward Medal as a sub-foreman at British Glues, Newark, in 1927.

William Lloyd, EM.

'On the night of the 3rd October, 1927, a man named Taylor was engaged in attending, at the works of Messrs Quibell Brothers Limited, a grease extracting plant used for extracting grease from bones by means of petroleum benzine. Noticing that benzine vapour was escaping from the extractor through the lid which had been incorrectly left open he endeavoured, with the help of a fellow workman, to close the lid. The fellow workman was affected by the fumes and on the suggestion of Taylor left the room. On recovering and finding later that Taylor had not followed him he gave the alarm.

William Lloyd, a sub-foreman of the works, who was not on duty but was passing the works on his way home, hearing that Taylor was in the building, put a scarf round his mouth and ran to the upper floor of the building where he found Taylor lying unconscious near the lid of the extractor. He succeeded in dragging Taylor down three steps to a lower floor, but was himself overcome and collapsed, and was later taken out of the building by other men.

Frank Boot, the foreman of the works, who had been summoned from his home, meanwhile arrived at the works, and, having put a handkerchief round his mouth, went into the building and found Taylor where Lloyd had left him. Boot then dragged Taylor to a point where other men could reach him, but he himself became affected with the fumes.

Lloyd and Boot, in rescuing Taylor, displayed a high degree of courage. It was stated in evidence at the inquest on Taylor, who did not survive, that at the time of the rescue the building was full of benzine fumes and that a cloud of fume was also visible outside the building. Apart from the risk of suffocation, there was the serious risk of an explosion, and both men were well aware of these risks.' (LG 9th December 1927)

Frank Boot was also awarded the Edward Medal.

Mr Lloyd served in the Home Guard during the Second World War and in later years he became a publican in Newark. He died at Newark on 16th June 1978, having received the Queen's Silver Jubilee Medal the previous year.

Bertram Frederick CROSBY, GC (formerly EM)

Bertram Frederick Crosby was born on 6th July 1912 and educated at Kingston Grammar School. He was a 16-year-old boy, living in Fleet Road, Hampstead, when he won the Edward Medal.

Bertie Crosby, GC, with his wife, Violet.

'About 10.40 am on the 9th of September 1927, a serious fire broke out at the premises of the Film Waste Products Limited, Redhill Street, Regent's Park. A quantity of cinematograph film which was being manipulated in a drying machine ignited without any warning, and the fire immediately spread to other film on adjacent benches and in other containers.

Crosby, who was then only 16 years of age, was passing through the drying room when the fire broke out. He at once ran to a door leading out into a yard, but on hearing a scream from near the drying machine he turned back into the room and made his way towards the machine, the contents of which were burning fiercely. He was unable to see anyone and he returned to the door leading into the yard. Here Crosby met the foreman and together, Crosby leading, they re-entered the room. As they made their way in, Crosby saw a girl fall up against one of the work tables, and he ran to her and half pulled and half carried her towards the door. Outside the door they both fell. Crosby was stupified by the heat and the fumes, and did not recover full consciousness until he found himself out in the yard with his clothes alight. He extinguished his clothes by the canal which ran at the bottom of the yard, and was subsequently removed to St Pancras Hospital.

The fire, which spread to another factory and two workshops, was particularly violent and resulted unfortunately in the death of five persons. Crosby could easily have escaped from the building without injury, but on two separate occasions he re-entered the room where the fire originated, in an endeavour to save life. The girl whom he helped out of the building afterwards died, and the burns sustained by Crosby were such that at one time it was not thought that he would recover.' (LG 15th May 1928)

Young Bertie also received an engraved watch from the Carnegie Hero Fund Trust and a five guinea (£5.25) cheque from the Society for the Protection of Life from Fire. Four years previously, he had saved his 3-year-old brother from drowning in Hampstead ponds. His investiture with the Edward Medal by the King took place at Buckingham Palace on 28th June 1928.

Mr Crosby was married and he and his wife, Violet, had three children. He had his own garage in Eton Avenue, Hampstead, until he retired in 1970. During the last war, he was in a reserved occupation, doing aircraft work. His father won the Distinguished Conduct Medal in the First World War.

Bertie Crosby died on 30th January 1972, aged 69.

John Thomas BAKER, GC (formerly EM)
James Sidney PURVIS, GC (formerly EM)

'A telephone message was received at the office of the South Garesfield Colliery, Durham, on 17th May 1929, that Richard Lowes, one of the Colliery deputies, had been injured during blasting operations. Robert Glendenning, an over-man, 55 years of age, set off down the pit and, collecting two lads, James Sydney Purvis and John Thomas Baker, at the bottom of the shaft, and a tram and stretcher, went in search of Lowes. They were joined by two hewers, John Kenny and Samuel Hughiff.

Meanwhile, five other men had been trying to rescue Lowes. Four of them were overcome by gas, while the fifth managed to crawl out just in time. It was on meeting this man some quarter of a mile from the scene of the accident that Glendenning realised the serious nature of the occurrence. He hurriedly organised his party and, by repeated efforts, they succeeded in extricating the five men who had been gassed, of whom three were dead.

The rescue party took such precautions as were possible at the time but first Kenny and then Hughiff were rendered unconscious. After they had, with difficulty, been removed from the danger area Glendenning sent Purvis for further help and continued the rescue work with the assistance of Baker. Baker was next overcome, and Glendenning was also affected by the fumes, but he continued his efforts until, when further help had arrived, he was able to bring out the last of the victims of the accident. He then collapsed and had to be carried out from the pit.

For an hour, during the whole of which time the atmosphere was thick with smoke and gas, Glendenning showed great courage and resource and displayed high qualities

John Baker, GC.   James Purvis, GC.

of organisation in directing the rescue operations. He himself, and Baker, Hughiff, Kenny and Purvis under his leadership, knowingly and repeatedly risked their lives in determined and sustained efforts to save the lives of their fellows, and there is no doubt that but for their courageous action the death-roll would have been heavier than it was.' (LG 22nd November 1929)

Robert Glendenning was awarded the Edward Medal in Silver and Samuel Hughiff and John Kenny the Edward Medal for their part in this incident.

John Thomas Baker was born on 14th April 1912 and educated at Leazes Elementary School, Burnopfield, near Gateshead in County Durham. He was a coalminer from 1926 to 1936. Mr Baker is married and he and his wife, Wendy, have one son.

He served as a regular soldier in the Royal Army Medical Corps from 1938 to 1945 in Palestine, Egypt, India, Iraq and Belgium, being awarded the 1939–45 Star, Africa Star, France and Germany Star, Defence Medal and War Medal. For his part in the above mentioned incident, he also received the Scouts' Bronze Cross and the Certificate of the Carnegie Hero Fund Trust.

After his war service, he went on the Reserve until 1950, his civilian employment being successively that of hotel chef from 1946–1952; work in a car factory, 1952–1960 and a boiler attendant from 1961 to 1977, when he retired. He received the Queen's Silver Jubilee Medal in 1977.

His hobbies are reading and all sports. He plays bowls occasionally. Mr Baker has lived in the Midlands since retirement and he elected to retain his original award of the Edward Medal in 1971.

James Sydney Purvis was born in Northumberland on 2nd July 1904 and educated at Leazes School. He became a miner in July 1918 and remained in that employment until July

126

1960. From then until 1969, when he retired, he was a maintenance labourer at the RHP Ballbearing Factory at Anfield Plain, County Durham.

Mr Purvis, who is now a widower, has two sons and his interests include gardening, billiards, snooker and greyhound racing. He was awarded the Queen's Silver Jubilee Medal in 1977 and now lives in retirement in County Durham. His EM was presented to the Imperial War Museum for display.

John William Hersey SHEPHERD, GC (formerly EM)

John William Hersey Shepherd was born on 20th December 1898 in County Durham and attended Dunn Street School, Jarrow. From 1913 to 1931, he worked for Palmers' Blast Furnaces in Jarrow.

During the last war, Mr Shepherd was in Civil Defence from 1939 to 1943, after which he became a steelworker at Jarrow Steel Works until his retirement. He won the Edward Medal for a most gallant attempt to save a colleague in 1929.

John Shepherd, GC, at his granddaughter's wedding.

'John Shepherd together with Hugh Black were detailed to clean a steam boiler at Palmers Shipbuilding and Iron Company Limited, Jarrow. On the 16th October 1929, Black entered the boiler and Shepherd was about to follow when he detected traces of gas. In reply to a call, he received only a faint reply from Black, and immediately climbed inside to go to his help. He found Black half conscious some twenty-five feet from the boiler manhole. He endeavoured to drag him to the opening but had to abandon the attempt as he was succumbing to the action of the gas. He made his way out of the boiler, called for help and, though still seriously affected by the gas, returned with a rope which he tried to fasten round his comrade who was then unconscious. He collapsed, however, before being able to do so.

Further assistance was procured. Compressed air was used to clear the gas out of the boiler, and eventually a rescue party wearing respirators succeeded in extricating both Black and Shepherd. Black unfortunately died a few hours later.

Twice during the course of the rescue operations Shepherd put his life in grave danger in a brave attempt to save the life of his fellow workman.' (LG 14th February 1930)

Mr Shepherd and his wife, Lily (née Moore) had eleven children – five boys and six girls, of

127

whom two girls and a boy are now deceased. His spare time interest was gardening and it is surprising how many of the miners in these pages followed this pastime.

John Shepherd was awarded the Queen's Silver Jubilee Medal in 1977 and died on 16th March 1983, aged 84.

Albert TYLER, GC (formerly EM)

Albert Tyler was born on 2nd April 1901 in Hertfordshire and attended the village school at Tewin. His principal employments were well sinker until *circa* 1946 and then thatcher and general contractor until retirement.

He won the Edward Medal under rather sad circumstances, as follows, in 1929.

'On the 19th October 1929, William Tyler and his two sons, Ernest and Albert, were engaged in cleaning and enlarging the cesspit of a factory at Burnham Green near Welwyn. Ernest Tyler, who had been lowered to the bottom of the pit by means of a bucket attached to a rope, became affected by gas and at his own request was being drawn up to the surface, but he fell out of the bucket when about twenty-two feet from the top of the pit. William Tyler at once descended to the rescue of his son but collapsed and became unconscious on reaching the bottom of the pit. In spite of the collapse of his father and brother which he had witnessed, Albert Tyler attempted to descend the pit and to rescue his relatives. He was driven back by the gas four times but at the fifth attempt he succeeded in reaching his father and brother and in passing a rope around them. They were hauled to the surface but artificial respiration and the administration of oxygen failed to revive them.

Albert Tyler proudly displays his EM and Royal Humane Society Silver Medal and Certificate.

Albert Tyler undoubtedly displayed great courage and determination in his attempts to save his father and his brother. The rescue operations lasted over a period of about forty minutes and every time he entered the pit he must have been fully aware that he was endangering his own life.' (LG 14th February 1930)

Mr Tyler was married with one daughter. He was a keen gardener and loved most sporting events. From 1930 until the late 1960s, he was a slipper for the North Herts Coursing Club. He died on 28th December 1975 and his Edward Medal went for display to Hertford Museum. The Royal Humane Society awarded him their Silver Medal for this incident and he also received the Certificate of the Carnegie Hero Fund Trust.

Granville Charles WASTIE, GC (formerly EM)

Granville Charles Wastie was born on 29th October 1902 in Oxfordshire and was educated at Witney Grammar School. He was a builder from 1916 to 1922 and then a farmer until retirement in 1974.

Mr Wastie was awarded the Edward Medal for a remarkably similar rescue to that of Albert Tyler (q.v.) and also, strangely, within twelve months of that same rescue.

'On the 25th November 1929, at North Leigh, Oxfordshire, Hector Wastie, a brick-layer, when descending a new well, thirty feet deep and three feet wide, was overcome by gas about half-way down and fell unconscious into thirty inches of water at the bottom. His brother Stanley went to his assistance but he too was rendered unconscious by the gas and collapsed. Another workman, George Broughton, attempted to descend

Granville Wastie, GC, with his family.

129

the well but when about half-way down he became faint and had to be pulled up by the rope which he had fastened around him. By this time Granville Wastie, a farmer, who had heard of the accident to his brothers, arrived in a motor car. After tying a handkerchief over his face and roping himself, he descended the well and, tying a rope round Stanley, succeeded in bringing him alive to the surface. Granville then went down a second time and brought up his other brother Hector. A doctor who was summoned found that Hector had been drowned after he had been rendered unconscious by inhaling carbon dioxide.

Granville Wastie displayed great courage in descending the well twice after three men had been overcome by gas and he almost certainly saved the life of his brother Stanley. He well understood the risk he was taking and exercised both skill and foresight in effecting the rescue.' (LG 6th and 10th June 1930)

This rescue, too, was tinged with tragedy, as will be seen from the above citation.

Mr Wastie is married with two sons, one of whom is serving in the army. He served in the Home Guard during the Second World War and was awarded the Queen's Silver Jubilee Medal in 1977. His hobbies are gardening and cricket.

After exchanging his Edward Medal, it was presented to the Ashmolean Museum in Oxford.

John Ingram GOUGH, GC (formerly EM)

Almost nothing is known of John Ingram Gough, who won the Edward Medal in 1929.

John Gough, GC, with his family at his reinvestiture.

'On the 11th September, 1929, two men, Redfern and Hardwick, were filling coal with other men at the Bretby Colliery, South Derbyshire, and were warned to leave their works as a shot was about to be fired near the place where they were working. As they were doing so about ten tons of roof fell and buried Redfern and Hardwick. Deputy Crofts and others at once tried, at great personal risk, to release the entrapped men. Although further falls were taking place, Crofts remained at work for twenty minutes trying to rescue Redfern until a further large fall of about 100 tons occurred and killed Redfern. Crofts was knocked down and bruised by this fall but he returned to the work of rescue and only gave up the attempt when he had crawled under the fall and had satisfied himself that Redfern was dead.

While Crofts was trying to release Redfern, Gough and others were attempting to free Hardwick. At great personal risk they removed the fallen coal from Hardwick's head and shoulders and placed over his body some covering timber which undoubtedly saved his life when the second large fall occurred.

During these operations the rescuers were several times compelled to take shelter from the falling material, and it was only after two hours work of an exceedingly dangerous nature that they succeeded in rescuing Hardwick alive and in recovering the body of Redfern.

Although all the rescue party showed great bravery and disregard for their own safety Crofts and Gough were recognised by their comrades to have been the most prominent in risking their lives.' (LG 17th June 1930)

Samuel Crofts also received the Edward Medal for his part in this incident.
Mr Gough died in Staffordshire on 23rd March 1977.

Arthur Devere THOMAS, GC (formerly EM in Silver)

Arthur Devere Thomas was born in Vancouver, British Columbia, on 1st October 1896. However, nothing is known of his early life or schooling.

He served in 28th Battalion of the Canadian Expeditionary Force in the First World War as a Private, earning the 1914–15 Star, British War and Victory Medals.

From 1931 to 1956, he worked for the Metropolitan Railway Company and then London Transport and soon after he commenced employment with the former, he won the Edward Medal in Silver.

'On the 14th January 1931, Ernest Percival, who was engaged in dismantling a wooden staging fixed across the track of the Metropolitan Railway Station at King's Cross,

Arthur Thomas, EM, being congratulated by his workmates. This illustration first appeared in *John Bull* magazine of 25th March 1933.

slipped and fell from a height of about twenty feet, to the permanent way of the down Inner Circle line. He was rendered unconscious and lay face downwards across one running rail with his head close to the negative rail of the electrified system.

Arthur Devere Thomas, who was acting as flagman for the pretection of the workmen, saw Percival fall and at the same time heard a down train approaching the station round the curve. Realising that a signal could not be seen by the driver in time for him to stop the train, Thomas immediately jumped down from the platform to the up line and, running across two positive and two negative rails carrying 600 volts, snatched Percival up from almost under the wheels of the approaching train, and held him, still unconscious, in a small recess in the wall whilst the train passed within a few inches of them. By reason of his employment,

Arthur Devere Thomas, GC, as an Inspector in the BTC Police.

Thomas must have been fully aware of the risks he faced and he displayed conspicuous gallantry in successfully effecting the rescue of Percival.' (LG 31st March 1931)

Subsequently, Mr Thomas joined the British Transport Police, retiring in 1956 as an Inspector. For his service during the Second World War, he held the Defence Medal and he was also awarded the Police Exemplary Service Medal.

Arthur Thomas died on 1st November 1973, at Harrow, Middlesex. He elected to retain his Edward Medal at the time of the exchanges.

Richard Henry KING, GC (formerly EM)

Richard Henry King was born on 13th January 1905 at Howdon-le-Wear, County Durham. However, when he was a small child, the family moved to the Stanley area and he was educated at Greenlands Infants and Junior Schools, South Moor, and what is now Anfield Plain Comprehensive School.

He became a miner in 1919 and, apart from a short period from 1936 to 1942 as a nurseryman, remained a miner until he retired in 1968.

Richard King was married and he and his wife, Ethel, had two sons and a daughter. They celebrated their golden wedding anniversary on 6th July 1982.

He was one of nineteen men to receive the Edward Medal for courage in 1930, one of these men being his own father, Victor King. However, he was the only survivor to exchange his medal for the George Cross.

Father and son, Victor and Henry King, who both won the Edward Medal in 1930, along with sixteen other men.

Richard Henry King, GC, and his wife on their Golden Wedding Anniversary; 6th July 1982.

'On the 29th September 1930, a fall of roof occurred in the Hedley Pit, South Moor, County Durham, partially burying a hewer, Frederick Beaumont. A chargeman, Victor King, was the first to come to the rescue. He found that a small passage-way remained open by which the buried man might be reached and, with the assistance of his son Richard and John George Tarn, he immediately built two chocks of timber to keep it open. The passage was seven yards long and about two feet square and the only practicable method of rescue was for three men to crawl along the passage-way and lie full length, two in the passage-way and one over Beaumont's body, and pass back, one at a time, the stones that were pinning him down.

This perilous and arduous work was carried on for nine hours by a team of miners (including Victor King) working in relays under the direction of the manager (Walter Robert Scott) and the under-manager (Robert Reed) until at last Beaumont was released, shaken but otherwise uninjured. During the whole nine hours the roof was shifting and "trickling" and on four occasions Beaumont was almost freed when a further fall buried him again. At one time the danger of a further fall appeared so great that the manager telephoned for the doctor (Dr Charles James Brookfield Fox) to come to the pit to amputate Beaumont's leg and so expedite his release. Fortunately – as it turned out – the doctor found it impossible to amputate in the restricted area in which Beaumont was confined, but he remained on the scene until Beaumont was rescued and examined and treated him before sending him to the surface.

Shortly after Beaumont was extricated the whole of the tunnel collapsed.' (LG 20th October 1931)

The other eighteen recipients of the Edward Medal were: John Thomas Akers, EM; Thomas Buckley, EM; Philip Cox, EM; John Dart, EM; Thomas Dixon, EM; Charles James Brookfield Fox, EM; Robert Johnston, EM; James Kent, EM; Victor King, EM; Joseph Lees, EM; George Forster Mason, EM; George Nancollas, EM; Robert Reed, EM;

Walter Robert Scott, EM; Walter Henry Sheldrake, EM; John George Tarn, EM; Thomas Henry Uren, EM; and William Waugh, EM.

All the above mentioned also received the Certificate of the Carnegie Hero Fund Trust. Mr King received the Queen's Silver Jubilee Medal in 1977.

His hobbies were reading, crosswords and gardening, with tomato growing as a speciality. He gave his Edward Medal to the Beamish Museum in County Durham.

Mr King died, aged 78, on 23rd November 1983.

Albert John MEADOWS, GC (formerly EM)

Albert John Meadows was born on 6th June 1904 and attended London County Council Schools. He was employed in the wine and spirits trade by Messrs W. A. Gilbey Ltd, for forty-seven years and won the Edward Medal for rescuing a colleague in 1931.

Albert Meadows, GC, with his wife Phyllis.

'On the 18th September 1931, John Gale, an employee at the distillery of Messrs W. A. Gilbey Limited, Camden Town, who was cleaning out with a hose pipe the residue in an empty cherry brandy vat, was discovered unconscious in the vat by his mate, Frederick Wormald, having apparently been gassed by the carbon dioxide generated by the fermentation of the residue. Wormald went down the ladder and tried unsuccessfully to get Gale out. He then called Leonard Wright, one the firm's analysts, and went down a second time, but was slightly gassed and had to be assisted out by Wright. Wright then went down himself but was overcome by the gas and became unconscious in the bottom of the vat. In the meantime, the Manager had sent for assistance, and Harold Hostler, a vatter, arrived on the scene and immediately entered the vat. He succeeded in dragging Wright to a sitting position near the foot of the ladder, but feeling himself being overcome by the fumes he was forced to come out of the vat. He made a second attempt with a wet cloth round his mouth and at a third attempt with a rope round his body he succeeded in getting Gale to the foot of the ladder and part of the way up, when he was overcome by the gas and Gale slipped from his grasp. Hostler himself was drawn up by the rope.

Albert Meadows (assistant store keeper) then volunteered to go into the vat, and at the second attempt, with a wet cloth round his mouth and a rope round his body, he succeeded in rescuing Wright. Although partially affected, he made a third but unsuccessful attempt to rescue Gale. He then asked for a length of rubber gas piping and

134

placing it in his mouth to breathe through and taking a looped rope with him, he went down a fourth time. He managed to place the rope round Gale and he and Gale were both drawn up from the vat. Wright and Gale recovered consciousness after an hour.

Both Hostler and Meadows displayed great courage and resource in their attempts to rescue the two men. Both were aware of the risks they were incurring, as two of the rescuers had already been overcome by the gas, and both took precautions calculated to render their attempts at rescue successful. They showed great persistence in facing deliberately what was a considerable risk. Hostler entered the vat three times and Meadows four times, and the periods occupied by their attempts at rescue were ten to fifteen minutes, and fifteen to twenty minutes, respectively.' (LG 29th December 1931)

Harold Henry Hostler was also awarded the Edward Medal.

During the Second World War, Mr Meadows served in the Royal Army Ordnance Corps, from 1942 to 1946, being demobilised as a Sergeant. He received the Queen's Silver Jubilee Medal in 1977.

Mr Meadows now lives quietly in retirement with his wife, Laura Phyllis, in Sussex, where he enjoys gardening and painting. A member of the Bognor Regis Art Society, he has exhibited paintings at the summer marquee exhibitions. Mrs Meadows is a member of the local WRVS Club.

Ernest ALLPORT, GC (formerly EM in Silver)
Richard Edward DARKER, GC (formerly EM)
Oliver SOULSBY, GC (formerly EM)
Frank SYKES, GC (formerly EM)
Samuel Jarrett TEMPERLEY, GC (formerly EM in Silver)
Philip William YATES, GC (formerly EM)

'At 5.45 in the afternoon of the 20th November last, a violent explosion of firedamp, followed by fires, occurred in the North East District of the Bentley Colliery, Yorkshire. Of some forty-seven persons working at or near the coal face, forty-five were either killed or died later. A large number of persons rendered heroic assistance in the work of rescue; and after careful investigation the eight* persons named appear to have displayed special gallantry.

Ward, pony driver, who was near an adjacent part of the coal face, was blown off his feet and enveloped in a thick cloud of dust, but as soon as he recovered himself went on his own initiative towards the face, guiding himself by rails and tubs, and assisted an injured man towards a place of safety. He repeatedly returned towards the face and helped to extricate injured men and bring them away; and he continued at rescue work for three hours, until completely exhausted. His bravery in groping his way towards danger, immediately after being knocked down by the blast, was outstanding. Darker,

---

*Edgar Hamilton Frazer and John Ward were also awarded the Edward Medal in Silver for their part in this gallant rescue.

Left to right: Philip Yates, Richard Darker, J. Ward, Frank Sykes and Oliver Soulsby at their investiture in 1932.

Forty years later. Left to right: Oliver Soulsby, Richard Darker, Frank Sykes, Philip Yates and Ernest Allport at their reinvestiture with the GC in 1972.

Soulsby, Sykes and Yates also displayed great gallantry and perseverance in extricating the injured and conveying them to a place of safety. It will be appreciated that the atmosphere was hot and vitiated and that there was evident risk of further explosions. One such explosion actually occurred at 10.30 pm injuring members of a rescue party, as mentioned below, and a third explosion occurred later.

Allport, Temperley and Frazer were prominently concerned with rescues from the area of the fires, which was explored somewhat later and in which the danger was extreme.

Temperley, an assistant surveyor at the colliery, volunteered to lead a rescue brigade to the return airway, where some men were still alive, by way of the face, there being a fire on the direct route. On the journey an explosion occurred severely burning three members of the party. The party then returned, but Temperley, though not equipped with breathing apparatus, went on, with one of the Mines Inspectors, as far as the entrance to the airway and subsequently helped to carry out an injured man past one of the fires and rendered other help. Allport, a member of the colliery Rescue Team, took a prominent part in the rescue operations, displaying energy, initiative and bravery, and encouraging other rescue men. He was over three hours in breathing apparatus and during part of the night, when his rescue apparatus required replenishing, he assisted in loading men on to stretchers. Subsequently, in answer to a call for volunteers after the second explosion, he seized a breathing apparatus, and joined a rescue party which penetrated past a fire to rescue two other men. Frazer, who is HM Divisional Inspector of Mines, explored much of the most dangerous area, displaying great gallantry in venturing among flames, smoke and afterdamp though not provided with a breathing apparatus; on hearing moaning in the return airway he ran back to summon a rescue party, but returned to the airway without waiting for them. He subsequently remained in the most dangerous area assisting to organise rescue operations and helped to take out past a fire two men rescued from the airway; and although exhausted he continued his efforts, until all the men, dead or alive, who were reported to be in the district had been extricated.' (LG 30th September 1932)

Ernest Allport was born on 10th April 1893 at Bolsover, Derbyshire and attended school there. The family, of whom there were eight boys and three girls, moved to Doncaster in 1908 and father and all eight sons were coal miners. Mr Allport began work on 10th April 1906 – his thirteenth birthday. He worked in the mines for fifty years, retiring through industrial injury in September 1956.

Mr Allport and his wife, Grace, had four children; three daughters and a son. In addition to the George Cross, Mr Allport holds the Queen's Silver Jubilee Medal 1977 and St John's Ambulance Long Service Medal, awarded to him as an Ambulance Officer in Doncaster Division, No 5 District. He had the Mines Rescue Medal and bar and was awarded the NCB Rescue Service Certificate for devotion to duty in the Mines Rescue Service from 1917 to 1944 – a remarkable record of service to others – on 7th April 1983.

His hobbies are walking and green bowling and he now lives quietly in retirement in Yorkshire. His EM was presented to Doncaster Museum.

Richard Edward Darker was born on 27th May 1910 and educated at the County Council Schools at Barton-on-Humber, Brigg and Redbourne. He became a coal miner at Markham Main Colliery, working there from 1925 to 1927, then moved to Bentley, where he remained until retirement in 1970.

Mr Darker and his wife, Edna May, have three children; two daughters and a son. Richard Darker enlisted into the Royal Engineers on 18th February 1943 but was discharged unfit as a result of the recurrence of illness from the Bentley explosion.

He holds the Queen's Silver Jubilee Medal 1977 and enjoys reading, sport, gardening and

Ernest Allport, GC, and his wife with the Mines Rescue Manager in 1983.

Richard Darker, GC.

Frank Sykes, GC.

Philip Yates at the time of his award.
Philip Yates, GC.

television. His Edward Medal was given to Doncaster Art Gallery and Museum when he exchanged it for the George Cross. He and his wife live in quiet retirement in Doncaster.

Oliver Soulsby was born in 1910 but nothing is known of his early life and schooling.

He won the Edward Medal in 1931, as outlined above.

Mr Soulsby died on 14th January 1977.

Frank Sykes was born at Bentley, Yorkshire, though the date is unknown, as are the details of his early life and schooling.

His Edward Medal was awarded in the circumstances outlined above.

Although Mr Sykes was invested with the George Cross, his Edward Medal was not surrendered for exchange and is believed to be still in circulation. He received the Queen's Silver Jubilee Medal in 1977 and died at Cleckheaton, Yorkshire, on 9th April 1982.

Philip William Yates was born in County Durham on 3rd January 1913 and went to Counden Church School, Bishop Auckland. He worked as an undertaker's assistant in 1926–27 before spending four years as a miner between 1927 and 1931 at various collieries. It was during this short period that he won his Edward Medal, as outlined above.

He is married with a son and a daughter and after the incident, he became a foundry worker until retirement. He received *The Daily Herald* Order of Industrial Heroism for the Bentley Colliery disaster.

His hobby is oil painting and today he lives in retirement in South Yorkshire. His Edward Medal is in Doncaster Museum and of course, in common with all surviving VC and GC recipients, he was awarded the Queen's Silver Jubilee Medal in 1977.

Samuel Jarrett Temperley was born on 21st August 1899 in County Durham and was educated in the local school at Rowlands Gill. He became a mining surveyor and engineer, was Assistant Surveyor at Bartley Colliery by 1925 and a Certificated Colliery Manager in 1930.

He served in the Durham Light Infantry in 1918 as a Private, being wounded in the left leg at Dickebusch, Belgium, and was awarded the British War and Victory Medals.

Mr Temperley was married to Mary Ivy Leighton and they had four children. He held a number of managerial posts with the NCB, including Deputy Area Production Manager, 1947–48; Area Production Manager, Carlton, Yorkshire, 1948–49; Area General Manager No 1 Area, Durham Division, 1953; Member, Doncaster Panel of Mining Examiners, 1946–50 and finally, President of the Yorkshire Branch, National Association of Colliery Managers, 1949–50.

Like his fellow EM recipients, he received the Certificate of the Carnegie Hero Fund Trust and was awarded the Queen's Silver Jubilee Medal in 1977.

Mr Temperley died on 15th December 1977, aged 78.

Samuel Temperley, GC.

Osmond WILLIAMS, GC (formerly EM)

Osmond Williams was born in North Wales on 20th January 1899 and educated at Friars School, Bangor, Caernarvonshire. He attended the University College of Bangor from 1920 to 1922, after service in the First World War as a Second Lieutenant in the Royal Field Artillery.

From 1925 to 1931, he was an oil engineer in Persia (now Iran) and in the latter year moved as an electrical foreman to Sierra Leone, where he was to win the Edward Medal.

'On the 15th July 1932, Mr Williams, an electrical foreman in the Public Works Department, Sierra Leone, received a telephone message to the effect that a distribution wire had fallen in a street in Freetown and he immediately went to investigate. When he arrived at the spot he saw a woman approaching the broken wire and shouted to her to stop, but she continued on her way and

Osmond Williams, GC.

140

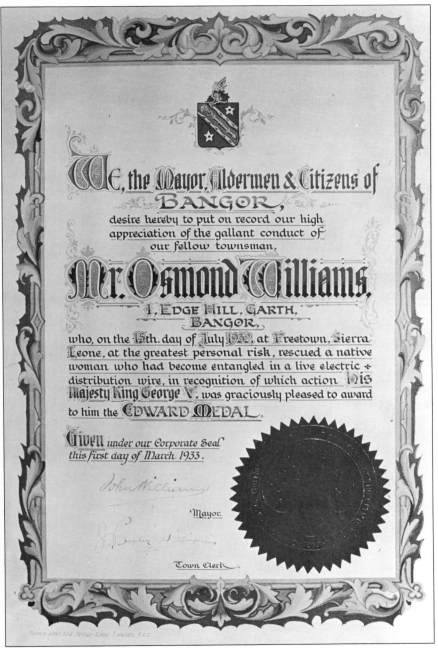

We, the Mayor, Aldermen & Citizens of BANGOR, desire hereby to put on record our high appreciation of the gallant conduct of our fellow townsman,

Mr. Osmond Williams,

1, EDGE HILL, GARTH,
BANGOR,

who, on the 15th. day of July 1932, at Freetown, Sierra Leone, at the greatest personal risk, rescued a native woman who had become entangled in a live electric & distribution wire, in recognition of which action his Majesty King George V. was graciously pleased to award to him the EDWARD MEDAL.

Given under our Corporate Seal this first day of March 1933.

John Williams

Mayor.

Town Clerk.

An illuminated scroll presented to Osmond Williams, GC.

became entangled in the wire. Mr Williams immediately endeavoured to free the woman and, in spite of severe shocks, succeeded in doing so. He applied artificial respiration until the woman's breathing appeared to be normal and then drove her to hospital. Afterwards he returned and superintended the repair of the broken wire. The woman subsequently died from the shock which she received. Mr Williams was an experienced electrician and, in consequence, was fully aware of the danger which he incurred. At the time, his clothing was wet with rain which greatly increased his peril, and there can be no doubt that he knowingly risked his own life in going to the woman's rescue.' (LG 29th November 1932)

As a result of this bravery, Mr Williams received an illuminated scroll of appreciation from the Mayor and Council of Bangor.

He continued to work in Sierra Leone until 1935. In 1939, he was recalled into the army and became Adjutant of the Royal School of Artillery at Larkhill, near Salisbury, retiring as a Major. He was married with two sons.

After the Second World War, Mr Williams returned to electrical engineering until 1968 and retirement. He received the Queen's Silver Jubilee Medal in 1977 and his hobbies were sketching and painting, photography and local history.

His Edward Medal is now at the Museum of the University College of Bangor, North Wales and he died on 4th March 1982, aged 82.

Thomas THOMAS, GC (formerly EM)

Thomas Thomas was born on 30th June 1912 in South Wales. He was educated at Garnant County Primary School and was employed as a coal miner from 1912 until 1960.

He won the Edward Medal for the following act of bravery in 1933.

'On the 21st September 1933, there was an inrush of water in the Brass Vein Slant of the Brynamman Colliery, Glamorgan. Thomas, a collier who was working underground at the time, assisted, at the risk of his own life, a youth who had lost his lamp and who was unable, in the darkness and rush of water, to make his way to safety, to reach a part of the working where several of the colliers had gathered. The colliers then divided into two

Thomas Thomas, GC.

groups seeking a way out by an airway and another group by a roadway which was flooded and obstructed by a mass of timber and rails which had been washed down by the water. Thomas took up the rear in the group that took the roadway, and when they succeeded in reaching safety he returned, at considerable peril to himself, to fetch the other group, who then escaped by the same route, Thomas being the last to leave.' (LG 6th February 1934)

Mr Thomas also received *The Daily Herald* Order of Industrial Heroism for this incident. He was awarded the Queen's Silver Jubilee Medal in 1977 and he and his wife, Margaret (née Davies) had one daughter. His hobbies were gardening and small-holding.

Mr Thomas gave his Edward Medal for display to the National Museum of Wales and he died on 19th July 1984, aged 72.

Norman BASTER, GC (formerly EM)
George William BEAMAN, GC (formerly EM)
James POLLITT, GC (formerly EM)

'On the evening of the 22nd August 1935, two explosions occurred at South Kirkby Colliery, Yorkshire, in a district about $1\frac{3}{4}$ miles from the shaft. It was thought that these were due to a gob fire and it was decided to seal off a part of the district by erecting stoppings.

At 3 pm on the 23rd August this work was in progress, and there were twenty-one men in the district, some near to the face and the others, of whom Beaman was one, at distances varying up to some 100 yards away. A further explosion then took place, severely injuring a number of the men. Beaman and two others, who had rescue apparatus, at once proceeded to look for and succour the injured, and with the assistance of others who followed shortly afterwards ten men were carried out of the district alive. One died almost immediately, eight within a few days, and one recovered. During the progress of these operations, which involved repeated journeys to and from the face, some of the rescuers who were not equipped with special apparatus were considerably affected by fumes.

It was found that everyone had been accounted for except a man named Dale; and although there was an increasing risk of a further explosion owing to accumulation of gas, search for him was renewed by Baster, who was the colliery agent, with the manager and four rescue men, including a man named Ball. They located Dale but he was found to be dead. They proceeded to remove his body, but while they were doing so a further explosion occurred and all six members of the party were burned. This explosion was severe enough not only to cause injury to the rescue party, who were comparatively near the face, but to affect those nearer the shaft who were looking after the men first injured. Baster got back and did what was possible to reassure these men and then with three others (of whom Beaman was one) he went in and removed Dale's body and later went in again for a certain distance to look for Ball, one of the rescue party injured by the second explosion, who was said to be missing. Baster, who had no apparatus, was this time so much affected by fumes and fatigue that he had to retire, but Beaman and another man conducted some further search without success. It was then reported that Ball had reached the shaft.

Later in the evening, however, after the rescue parties had left the mine, it was found that Ball was after all still missing. There were reasons for fearing that a further

Norman Baster, GC.

George Beaman, GC.

James Pollitt in 1935.

explosion might shortly occur and that a fresh search might only swell the casualty roll; but volunteers were anxious to descend the mine and make a further attempt, and one of the rescue parties so formed entered the district and succeeded in finding Ball and bringing him safely to the surface. In this final operation, which was conducted at once with determination and prudence, J. Pollitt acted as captain of the rescue party.

Great courage and pertinacity were displayed by many others who took part in these operations and it has not been easy to discriminate between those concerned, but it is considered that Beaman rendered services of outstanding merit in the first stage, Baster in the second stage and Pollitt in the final stae of the rescue operations.' (LG 17th April 1936)

Norman Baster was born in Hampshire on 11th January 1892 and educated at Eastleigh. He attended the University of London from 1911 to 1913 and the University of Nottingham from 1919 to 1923. He served in the Royal Engineers during the First World War, in the European theatre of operations earning the 1914–15 Star, British War and Victory Medals. He rose to the rank of Colonel and served once again during the Second World War in the Home Guard.

His civilian occupation was mining engineer and his hobby is collecting pewter. Mr Baster

James Pollitt (centre) as captain of the South Kirby Mines Rescue Team in 1939.

received the Queen's Silver Jubilee Medal in 1977 and now lives in retirement in Canada.

George William Beaman was born on 25th January 1904 at Sheffield in Yorkshire. He was educated at Netherthorpe Council and St Paul's Church of England Schools, Sheffield. For a short time, 1917–21, he was a silversmith but in 1921, he became a miner and deputy, a calling he followed until 1948. From that date until retirement in 1969, he was a builder.

Mr Beaman married Ada, née Cracknell and they had seven children of whom four survive.

He served in the Royal Air Force from 1939 to 1942, being an Aircraftman First Class but he was released for mines rescue. In addition to the George Cross, he holds the Defence Medal, War Medal and Queen's Silver Jubilee Medal 1977. His EM is now on display at the Council Chambers, Hemsworth, Yorkshire. His hobbies are St John's Ambulance and First Aid. Mr Beaman now lives in Australia.

James Pollitt was born in Wigan on 2nd December 1896 and attended Whelley Church of England School, followed by Wigan Mining and Technical College. As a mining student, he was offered a scholarship to Oxford to study maths but declined, owing to the shortage of jobs at that time. He went to work in the mines, where he eventually became a manager. He was also a mines rescue team captain and it was in this capacity that he won the Edward Medal.

Mr Pollitt was married in 1934 to his wife, Mary Jane, a lady widowed in the First World War, and they had one daughter. His wife and daughter nursed him during his final illness, until he died on 8th September 1972, aged 75.

Although he handed in his Edward Medal, he had not received the George Cross at the time of his death. He was looking forward to going to Buckingham Palace to be re-invested. He and his wife were keen Royalists and his original investiture was at the only one held by King Edward VIII during that monarch's short reign.

George Christopher HESLOP, GC MC (formerly EM)

George Christopher Heslop was born on 25th December 1885 but nothing is known of his early life and schooling. He served as an officer in the Durham Light Infantry during the First World War, rising to the rank of Captain and winning the Military Cross.

He won the Edward Medal for his endeavours to save two lives in a Yorkshire mine in 1935.

George Heslop, MC, EM.

'At about 8.30 am on the 17th December, 1935, a fall of roof occurred at the Loftus Ironstone Mine, Yorkshire, and two workmen, John Cooper Henry and Henry Murrell, were buried in the debris. Mr Heslop, who is the Agent and Manager of the mine, arrived on the scene at about 9.00 am and although falls were still occurring and there was considerable roof movement so that the workers in the mine had not ventured to go to the rescue of the two men, Mr Heslop crawled for about four yards under the fall into a cavity of about two feet until he reached Henry, from whose face he removed stones, but whom he was unable to free as there was a baulk across his legs. He then instructed the men to pile a road through the fall to protect Henry from further falls and to expedite his release. Afterwards he again crawled under the fall, a distance of three to four yards, and located Murrell who was pinned by one of his feet. Mr Heslop gave him a stimulant and then worked strenuously for four hours in a cavity so small that there was room for only one person, until he liberated him alive. Falls were continually occurring and he was in such danger that workmen and officials repeatedly urged him to withdraw. After Murrell was released, Mr Heslop again crawled into the cavity to Henry and supervised the cutting of the runner baulk by which he was pinned and was able to release him alive after he had been imprisoned for eight hours. Shortly after there was a heavy fall and the whole of the piling which had been erected to assist in his release collapsed.

In rescuing these men (both of whom unfortunately died later of shock) Mr Heslop showed outstanding courage and was exposed to very great personal risk.' (LG 26th May 1936)

Mr Heslop also received the Bronze Medallion of the Carnegie Hero Fund Trust for this rescue. He was awarded the Queen's Silver Jubilee Medal in 1977 and died at Saltburn-by-the-Sea in December 1978.

Robert Benjamin SAUNDERS, GC, MB, ChB (formerly EM)

Robert Benjamin Saunders was born in 1905, although the exact date and place are unknown, as are details of his early life and education.

However, he went on to qualify as a Doctor of Medicine and it was in this capacity that he won the Edward Medal in Southern Rhodesia in 1937.

'On the 4th January, 1937, an accident occurred in the Tebekwe Mine, Salisbury, Southern Rhodesia, in which one of the miners – a man named Sheasby – was trapped underground by a fall of rock and completely buried.

Dr Saunders arrived on the scene at 3.15pm, by which time the rescue party had succeeded in removing most of the spillage from the imprisoned man's body. It was found, however, that his left hand was firmly held between two timbers. He remained in this dangerous position until 12.30pm the following day.

During the whole of this time (with the exception of a short interval when he went to the surface for some food) Dr Saunders remained underground rendering every medical assistance under extremely difficult and dangerous conditions. The situation of the imprisoned man was such that, in order to attend his patient at all, the doctor had to lie on top of him with his back in close proximity to a dangerously shaky roof, any disturbance of which would have resulted in a fall sufficient to crush them both.

After a period of sixteen hours, when all efforts to extricate the miner had failed, it was decided to amputate his arm. The conditions only allowed of left-handed work and the operation was therefore performed by a left-handed amputator under the personal supervision of Dr Saunders. Sheasby was then transported to the surface, and has now completely recovered from the effects of his long ordeal.

Dr Saunders displayed great devotion to duty in circumstances of grave danger, and his example undoubtedly inspired the injured man with fortitude and the rescuers with courage and determination.' (LG 8th October 1937)

Doctor Saunders was awarded the Queen's Silver Jubilee Medal in 1977 and died on 14th September 1981.

David Noel BOOKER, GC (formerly EM)
Samuel BOOKER, GC (formerly EM)

'On the afternoon of 14th May 1937, three men were at work dismantling the plant at a conveyor face in a gate, at a distance of some seventy or eighty yards from the main level, in the Littleton Colliery, South Staffordshire. Firedamp appeared to be spreading in the gate, since, at about 8pm, a fireman set off from the level to see what the men were doing up the gate and found that his lamp was extinguished at about twenty yards from the level. Between this time and about midnight, when full rescue apparatus became available and the bodies were recovered, efforts at rescue were made by a succession of men, some of whom themselves collapsed and thereby added to the task of later rescuers; of these one, Mr Walmsley, the Under-Manager, himself lost his life, thus bringing the death roll to four. In these operations the brothers Booker were outstanding. Each of them forced his way up the gate on four or five separate occasions,

David Booker pictured on his wedding day in 1936.

David Booker and his wife at his reinvestiture.

and they were jointly or severally responsible for extricating four earlier rescuers who had succumbed to the gas; all of these survived except Mr Walmsley, the Under-Manager. On all of these occasions the brothers Booker, who seem to have been men of high resisting powers, displayed great courage, which is to be rated even more highly as it was reinforced by an almost equal measure of coolness and forethought.' (LG 4th February 1938)

David Noel Booker was born in Staffordshire on 19th October 1910 and educated at Bloxwich Church of England School. He became a coal miner in 1923, leaving the mines in 1957, when he was employed with the North Midlands Passenger Transport Executive. He retired from this job, due to illness, on 16th November 1974.

Samuel Booker on his wedding day.

He and his wife, Jane, had two children, a son and a daughter. His hobbies were gardening· and woodwork. David Booker died at Walsall, West Midlands, on 30th March 1982, aged 71. He was awarded the Queen's Silver Jubilee Medal in 1977 and although invested with the George Cross, his Edward Medal was never returned to the Home Office.

Almost nothing is known of Samuel Booker, not even the date of his birth. He won the Edward Medal with his brother, David Noel, as outlined above.

Mr Booker received the Queen's Silver Jubilee Medal in 1977 and he died in about 1981.

Azariah CLARKE, GC, BEM (formerly EM)

Not much is known about Azariah Clarke, who was probably born between 1895 and 1897. He served in the First World War.

Mr Clarke won the Edward Medal for courage in 1937 during the following incident:

Azariah Clarke, GC, BEM.

'On the 2nd July, 1937, at about 5.45 am a fire started in the holing of the Four Foot Seam at Holditch Colliery, North Staffordshire. The fire spread rapidly but of the fifty-five men employed in the affected area at the time all except two succeeded in withdrawing from the danger zone. As soon as it was found that the two men were missing, an unsuccessful search was made for them. At 6.50 am an explosion occurred and one of the search party was afterwards found to be missing. Meanwhile a call for the Colliery Rescue Brigade had gone out, and by 7.30 am Azariah Clarke had assembled three others at the pithead and proceeded to lead them below ground. The party met the managing director of the colliery in the neighbourhood of the fire, and he instructed them to search for the man who had been lost after the explosion. They accordingly donned their breathing apparatus and started on their search in the direction of the face. The atmosphere was hot, dusty and foul with gas and smoke, and on reaching a fall which blocked the way into the face they retraced their steps, continuing meanwhile to search for the missing man, but without success.

The Rescue Brigade – now increased to five by the arrival of another member – next went to search for the two men who had been lost at the time of the original fire. Still using their breathing apparatus, they stumbled in the smoke up a steep road, parts of which had a gradient of 1 in 2½ to 1 in 3. Soon after 10 am, while they were thus engaged, a severe explosion occurred resulting in the deaths of twenty-seven persons most of whom had been sent down for the purpose of erecting stoppings to seal off the fire. The Rescue Brigade were but slightly affected by this explosion and, having made their way to a telephone, they arranged to come out to secure fresh breathing apparatus since their supplies of oxygen were running low.

During the period of some two hours, during which the Brigade had been searching for the lost men under Clarke's leadership, they had survived two other explosions of lesser intensity (as well as the major explosion to which reference has been made) and had been working throughout in conditions of the greatest difficulty and danger with the realisation, moreover, that further explosions might occur at any moment.

Having secured new apparatus Clarke again led the Brigade into the danger zone. Travelling down the road over falls of ground and derailed tubs, and past other debris produced by the explosion, and extinguishing a fire encountered on the way, they came upon a number of badly injured men and dead bodies. They made the injured as comfortable as possible, and arranged for stretchers to be sent in.

On the arrival of further assistance some members of the Rescue Brigade helped in evacuating the injured and the dead while Clarke and others made a further examination of the workings with a view to ensuring that no living person had been left behind. By 3.25 pm all the men known to be alive had been recovered, and as it was thought that there was a considerable risk of a further explosion all the men were withdrawn from the mine. The Rescue Brigade had worked almost continuously in breathing apparatus since 7.30 am. Later on doubt arose as to whether there might still be some injured persons alive in the pit, and at 6 pm Clarke again led a brigade down the mine. After an exhaustive search they found no live men below, and returned to the surface at 8.30 pm. In view of the serious nature of the brigade's report on the conditions in the mine it was decided that no more men should be allowed to go down until the fire area had been flooded.

The courage, initiative, endurance and qualities of leadership displayed by Clarke throughout these lengthy operations were outstanding.' (LG 5th August 1938)

Mr Clarke, who also held the British Empire Medal, died at Newcastle-under-Lyme, Staffordshire, on 17th February 1975.

Benjamin Littler JONES, GC (formerly EM)

Benjamin Littler Jones was born in North Wales on 13th July 1918 and attended Llysfaen School and Colwyn Bay High School. After leaving school, Ben Jones went to work in the Llanddulas Quarry, between Abergele and Old Colwyn.

'Blasting was about to take place at the Llysfaen quarry, Caernarvonshire, on the morning of the 21st May 1938. All the men with the exception of three, Williams, Jones and Roberts, whose duty it was to light the fuses, had been withdrawn from the danger zone. Williams had lighted one fuse, Jones two and Roberts three when Roberts trod on a stone which tipped up and trapped his foot so that he could not move. The shots were timed to go off in eighty seconds, and Roberts was in imminent danger of being killed. Williams and Jones tried to release Roberts, and failing to do so, Williams shouted to the others to pull out the fuses and promptly pulled out four himself. Jones pulled out one and Roberts the other. In doing so they ran a considerable risk; had any one of the detonators exploded, it would certainly have had serious or even fatal results. The promptitude and courage of Williams and Jones undoubtedly saved the life of Roberts at grave risk to their own safety.' (LG 9th September 1938)

William Williams also received the Edward Medal for this incident.

When he was twenty, on 21st December 1938, Ben Jones joined the Royal Air Force, serving throughout the Second World War until 19th July 1947, being discharged as Flight Sergeant. He served overseas from 4th June 1945 to 19th July 1947.

He was married on 12th June 1943 and he and his wife, Mary Ellen, had five children; two sons and three daughters. One son is now deceased.

Mr Jones declined to exchange his Edward Medal for the George Cross and he held the Defence and War Medals for his war service in the RAF. The Institute of Quarrying awarded him its medal for bravery.

For hobbies, he enjoyed football, tennis, darts and billiards.

He died at Colwyn Bay, Clwyd, on 8th August 1975, aged 57.

Ben Littler Jones, EM. He is wearing the medal of the National Association of Quarrymen.

Ernest William KENT, GC (formerly EM)

Ernest William Kent was born on 2nd August 1914. Nothing is known of his early life but in 1938, he was engaged on construction work in London when he won his Edward Medal.

'On the night of the 25th October 1938, gangs of workmen were engaged in concrete piling work at the Hackney Wick Stadium. Metal cylinders about fifteen inches in internal diameter were being sunk into the ground, the earth inside them being then removed. At about 2.30 am a gang of three workmen under the charge of Herbert William Baker encountered an obstruction at the bottom of one of these cylinders, which had been sunk to a depth of some eighteen feet. Baker, who was a small man, decided to have himself lowered down the cylinder, presumably with the idea of clearing the obstruction with his feet. He was advised against doing so by one of the workmen who said that he smelt gas, but Baker persisted and was lowered feet foremost into the shaft hanging with out-stretched arms on the hook of the winch rope. When he was about twelve feet down he shouted for help and the men began to pull him up, but before he reached the top he lost his grip on the hook and fell to the bottom. Messages for help were sent but in the meantime Kent, one of the labourers, who was also a small man, volunteered to be lowered head first down the cylinder in an attempt to pull Baker up with his hands. His feet were lashed to the winch cable and he was lowered head first for some distance but then gave signs of distress and was hauled up in a state of semi-collapse and bleeding from the mouth. In the meantime the Fire Brigade and

Police had arrived and an oxygen cylinder with the jet partially turned on was lowered to a position near Baker's head in an effort to improve the atmosphere until a rescue could be effected. The ground surrounding the cylinder was also dug away to enable the upper 3-foot section to be unscrewed, thus reducing the depth to about fifteen feet. These operations had taken over an hour and it was realised that there was no chance of getting Baker out alive by these means. A call was made for a volunteer small enough to descend the shaft and another workman volunteered and was lowered head first into the cylinder. A short distance from the top, however, a ridge round the inside of the tube jammed his shoulders and he had to be drawn up again. Kent, who during this time had partially recovered from the effects of his first rescue attempt then volunteered to

Ernest Kent, GC.

make a further effort, and as there appeared to be no other chance of freeing Baker alive his offer was accepted and he was again lowered into the shaft. He succeeded in grasping Baker and as he was drawn up he was heard to be gasping for breath and called out, "Quick, Quick." He just had sufficient strength to retain his grip until helpers round the shaft top caught Baker's arms when he collapsed, practically unconscious. Both men were taken to Hospital, but it was found that Baker was dead.

Kent showed great initiative and courage in his two efforts to rescue Baker. He was secured by a rope, but there was a serious risk of his becoming jammed in the narrow cylinder at a depth from which it would have been difficult, if not impossible, to extricate him, and there was also a grave risk of suffocation. The time occupied in his second attempt was about four or five minutes. It is clear that he risked his own life in his attempts – unhappily not successful – to save the life of his fellow workman.' (LG 20th December 1938)

Mr Kent also received the Bronze Medallion of the Carnegie Hero Fund Trust and the Royal Humane Society's Medal for this act.

He was married with three daughters and was an electrician in his spare time. During the last war, he served in the army, from July 1940 to 1946, attaining the rank of Corporal. His civilian job after the war was as a millwright at Ford of Dagenham.

Ernest Kent died at Basildon, Essex, on 23rd August 1973, aged 69.

152

A reinvestiture at Buckingham Palace. Fred Haller, GC, is on the extreme right of the group.

Fred HALLER, GC, BEM (formerly EM)

Fred Haller was born in 1892 at Rossington, near Doncaster and spent all his life there. From 1906 to 1913 he was an apprentice carpenter, earning 3/- (15p) per week. He then went to work at Rossington Colliery. He married Helen Dobb and they had a son and a daughter. He served in the First World War.

It was as a Deputy at Rossington that he won the Edward Medal.

'An abandoned heading in Rossington Main Colliery, Yorkshire, had been fenced off as dangerous on account of gas. About 1.30 am on the 8th October 1938, a driver named Dakin, employed with a contractor named Godfrey and his son in enlarging the road, was missed. Planks composing the fence which shut off the dangerous heading were found to have been pulled on one side and a light was seen some distance up the heading. Godfrey and his son concluded that Dakin must have entered the heading for some reason and got into difficulties, so the son went for assistance. A man named Durkin arrived first, followed by Haller, the Deputy for the District, and another Deputy. Godfrey had turned on a compressed air hose but it failed to reach the fence by two yards. Haller sent for more hosepipe, and taking a singlet which Godfrey had saturated with water went up the heading to try and rescue Dakin. He could see that Dakin was some forty yards beyond the fence, and he knew that the atmosphere in the heading was likely to be irrespirable, as he had been present a few weeks previously

153

when tests made in the heading revealed the presence in large quantities of methane and carbon dioxide. As a trained Deputy, Haller was able to appreciate the risk he was running by venturing over forty yards up an incline of one in seven, without breathing apparatus of any description, through such an atmosphere. Advancing cautiously up the heading, so as not to exhaust himself, he reached Dakin who was unconscious and with considerable effort succeeded in dragging him up to the fence where he arrived in an exhausted condition. It was some hours before Dakin recovered complete consciousness after the application of artificial respiration, and there is no doubt that if the rescue had been delayed he would have been asphyxiated.' (LG 20th January 1939)

Mr Haller also received the Certificate of the Carnegie Hero Fund Trust and a cash award for his bravery. Eight years later, he was awarded the British Empire Medal for risking his life while trying to save a colleague buried by a rock fall (LG 4th February 1947). He suffered a broken leg in this second incident, which finished his career underground and he became a Safety Officer at the pit top.

In 1977, he was awarded the Queen's Silver Jubilee Medal. An all-round sportsman, he enjoyed football, cricket, billiards and he was at one time a champion cyclist.

He died, aged 92, on 17th September 1983.

Robert Stead LITTLE, GC (formerly EM)

Robert Stead Little was born on 23rd June 1892 in Manchester and educated at Birley Street School. He worked for ICI at Blackley, Manchester.

Robert Little, GC, with his family, outside Buckingham Palace, 3rd March 1973.

'On the 11th January 1939, a fitter engaged on repairs in a chemical reaction pan at the works of the British Dyestuffs Corporation at Blackley, Manchester, fell into the pan. Little, who was in charge of the shift, was called and while rescue apparatus was being brought, he descended into the pan at great risk to himself and carried his unconscious fellow-worker up the ladder. Unfortunately, however, another man who had started to go down the manhole collapsed on the top of Little and the rescued man, knocking them both to the bottom where all three remained unconscious. The rescue party then arrived and brought them to the surface. Two of them were dead, but Little recovered.' (LG 5th May 1939)

He served in the First World War as a Private in the Lancashire Fusiliers, being awarded the 1914–15 Star, British War and Victory Medals. In later years he lived on Merseyside with his wife, Jessie. They had no children. He received the Bronze Medallion of the Carnegie Hero Fund Trust for his brave act.

Mr Little, whose hobbies were cricket and football, died on 31st May 1976, at Wallasey, Merseyside, aged 83.

Bernard FISHER, GC (formerly EM)

Bernard Fisher was born on 14th December 1911. He went to work in the steel industry as a crane driver in 1927 and in 1954 became crane foreman, a position he held until retirement on 30th September 1974.

He won the Edward Medal in 1939 in the following circumstances:

Bernard Fisher, GC, with his GC and EM.

'In the early morning of 26th April 1939, a fire occurred in the cabin of an electrically driven gantry crane running at a height of about fifty-five feet above ground level in the Templeborough Steel Melting Shop of Messrs Steel, Peech & Tozer Ltd, Sheffield. The driver – William Hird – shouted and then lost consciousness. Fisher, who was the driver of a travelling jib crane in the same department, heard the shout and saw the fire. He promptly climbed from his own box and ascended the ladder to the crane track. He crossed the eighty feet span of the gantry and descended the vertical ladder into the cabin, which by that time was blazing. He carried Hird through a trap door and up a vertical ladder for a distance of approximately twelve feet. Fisher's action, which was carried out at great risk to himself and showed intelligence and initiative, almost certainly saved Hird's life.' (LG 15th August 1939)

He was invested with his medal on 6th February 1940 at Buckingham Palace by King George VI and was presented with a gold watch and chain by colleagues in the industry.

Mr Fisher and his wife, Elsie Annie, have one son.

On 17th July 1974, he was invested with the George Cross and presented his EM to Clifton Park Museum, Rotherham, Yorkshire. He received the Queen's Silver Jubilee Medal in 1977 and enjoys gardening as a hobby. He now lives in retirement in South Yorkshire.

ORDER of INDUSTRIAL HEROISM

INSTITUTED BY
The Daily Herald
Presented as a mark of
respect and admiration
to *John Dixon*
a brave man who in a
moment of peril thought
more of others than of
himself

date 31st January 1940

The certificate awarded by *The Daily Herald* to accompany the Order of Industrial Heroism.

John DIXON, GC (formerly EM)

John Dixon was born on 23rd June 1913 at Bradford, Yorkshire, the fourth child of ex-QMS Frederick Dixon, King's Own Yorkshire Light Infantry, a veteran of the North West Frontier of India and Boer War. The family moved to Grantham in late 1914, when Mr Dixon senior was appointed Barrack Warden at Belton Camp until 1920, then Harrowby Camp. They moved to Lincoln when Dixon senior was appointed Barrack Warden at New Barracks (now Sobraon Barracks).

John Dixon attended school at St John's Infants Junior, Spittlegate, Grantham; Westgate Junior and North District Intermediate Schools, Lincoln.

After school, John Dixon went to work for Robey and Co Ltd, Globe Works, Lincoln, where he stayed until 1953, joining Leys Malleable Castings Ltd, Lincoln, in that year, remaining until 1955. From 1955 until 1978, when he retired as an Electrical Chargehand, he worked for Ruston and Hornsby of Lincoln.

It was while working for Robey and Co that he won the Edward Medal.

'On the 16th February 1939, an accident occurred during the casting of a mould at the foundry of Messrs Robey and Company Limited, Globe Works, Lincoln, which resulted in two large overhead electric cranes and the foundry roof being set on fire. Dixon, who is an electrician, was on the crane gantry to watch the electrical equipment and was able to escape from immediate danger, but the driver of one of the cranes, a man named Whittaker, who managed to climb out of the cabin, collapsed on the top of the crane with his clothing ablaze. Dixon saw this and promptly went back to rescue Whittaker, although the fire was then at its height and there was also some risk of his suffering an electric shock. He extinguished the flames from Whittaker's clothing and carried him from his own crane across the crane in the next bay, out on to the roof gutter, along and then across the roof, and down a vertical ladder, thirty-one feet in length, to the ground. Dixon then collapsed. He was very badly burned about the arms and upper part of the body and was absent from work about ten weeks. His action, which involved going back from a point of comparative safety to face considerable risk, almost certainly saved Whittaker's life.' (LG 23rd February 1940)

John Dixon, GC, shows his father's medals for service in Africa and India.

John Dixon married Edith Ethel Scott on 8th January 1933, at Thomas Cooper Memorial Baptist Church, Lincoln. His spare time interests include do-it-yourself, assisting in the care of the elderly and chess. He also takes great pride in representing the Victoria Cross and George Cross Association at both the Battle of Britain Service and the Remembrance Service held annually in Lincoln Cathedral.

He received a number of awards for his brave rescue of Mr Whittaker, including the Bronze Medal of the Society for the Protection of Life from Fire, £50 cheque and Certificate of the Carnegie Hero Fund Trust, *The Daily Herald* Order of Industrial Heroism and a Westminster chiming clock and purse from the workmen, staff and directors of Robey and Co Ltd.

Mr Dixon was invested with the George Cross in November 1972 and his Edward Medal is now in the City and Country Museum, Lincoln. He now lives in retirement in Lincoln.

Matthew THOMPSON, GC, BEM (formerly EM)
Charles SMITH, GC (formerly EM)

'At 10 am on the 3rd January 1940, a fall of roof occurred at a coal face in Warren House Seam at Askern Main Colliery, Yorkshire, and a miner named Charles Liversidge was buried by the fall. He was extricated some three hours later, without having suffered serious injury, through the gallantry displayed, in conditions of the greatest risk, by a rescue party.

From the *Evening Standard* of 2nd July 1940, left to right, Matthew Thompson, Charles Smith and Gwyn Morgan.

Morgan, the Agent of the Colliery, arrived a few minutes after the accident and took charge of the operations. With great difficulty a way was cleared under the fall, and it was found that Liversidge was completely buried, except for his head and shoulders, and that his arms were pinned by fallen rocks and by a steel bar. Morgan succeeded in removing a stone which was pinning one of his arms. Later, when one of the other men had failed, he succeeded in getting through to Liversidge and after thirty minutes' work in the most cramped position was able to free him and to pass him through to the other rescuers. Throughout he displayed outstanding courage, resource and leadership.

Smith and Thompson were both close at hand when the fall occurred and at once commenced rescue operations. They took a prominent part in the dangerous work of clearing a way under the fall, and both were able to remove some of the debris which had pinned Liversidge down. Thompson attempted to get through to effect the final release of Liversidge, but was driven back by a further fall.

The whole work of rescue was carried on in the most difficult and dangerous conditions, and slight falls occurred frequently.

A further heavy fall occurred later in the day which completely closed the passage through which the rescue had been made.' (LG 28th June 1940)

Gwyn Morgan was awarded the Edward Medal in Silver for this rescue.

Matthew Thompson was born on 24th January 1898 in County Durham and went to school at Etherley, near Bishop Auckland. He spent all his working life in the coal industry, first in Durham then at Askern in Yorkshire.

He was invested with the Edward Medal on 2nd July 1940 and opted not to exchange it for

158

The King decorates Charles Smith, Matthew Thompson and Gwyn Morgan with the EM.

Charles Smith, EM, while serving with
the Royal Artillery.

Charles Smith, GC, as he is today.

the George Cross in 1971. *The Daily Herald* awarded him its Order of Industrial Heroism.

Mr Thompson held the post of Branch Secretary of Askern NUM from 1942 to 1962 and was a Welfare Trustee from 1962 until 1976. Other appointments he held were member of Askern Parish Council, Doncaster RDC and Alderman of the West Riding County Council from 1942 to 1971. He was a Justice of the Peace and received the British Empire Medal in the Queen's Birthday Honours of 1955 – a remarkable record.

He was married with two children, both boys. His wife was Margaret Alice (née Moore). Mr Thompson was awarded the Queen's Silver Jubilee Medal in 1977 and died in hospital on 19th April 1981, aged 83.

Charles Smith was born on 17th December 1908 and attended St William's RC School, Ince, near Wigan, Lancashire. He went to work in the pits in 1921 and remained working underground until 1940.

From 1940 to 1945, he served in the Royal Artillery, being awarded the 1939–45 Star, Burma Star, Defence and War Medals and attaining the rank of Sergeant. He was awarded the Queen's Silver Jubilee Medal in 1977.

He married Louisa Turner, who died in 1977, and they had a son and a daughter. His hobbies, when younger, were boxing, motorcycling and long-distance running but in later years, he lists sport and gardening as his interests.

From 1945 to 1961, Mr Smith was a surface worker at Stargate Colliery, Ryton-on-Tyne and in the coking industry from 1961 to 1973 at Derwenthaugh. He retired in December 1973 and now lives quietly in Tyne and Wear.

Thomas JAMESON, GC (formerly EM)
Carl Mallinson SCHOFIELD, GC (formerly EM)

'About 8.45 pm on the 14th February 1940, a serious fall of roof occurred in the main loading level of the Bold Colliery, Lancashire, completely burying five men. Rescue operations were immediately begun and in 1¼ hours one of the men was liberated and was able to walk out of the pit with assistance. He was able to tell the agent, Thomas Jameson, who had arrived and taken charge, the approximate position of the other four men. Jameson, assisted by a night shift foreman, Carl Schofield, whose father was one of the men buried, working only with their hands (there was no room for a shovel) removed stones and dirt and sawed through a conveyor chain and a rail, and after prolonged efforts one of the men was rescued by 2 am next morning. Operations were continued, other men taking turns, until about 3 am a third man was released. The other two men could be seen but appeared to be dead.

The rescue had to be carried out in a very confined space and in conditions of extreme difficulty and danger owing to the imminent risk of further falls as the debris which covered the burried men was removed. If this had not been prevented by the skilful directions of Jameson the number of deaths would almost certainly have been greater. Immediately after the third man had been released there was another big fall which completely blocked the hole which the rescuers had been using as a means of access.

The rescues were undoubtedly due to the coolness, courage and skilful leadership of Jameson and to the assistance he received from Schofield, who displayed the greatest

Thomas Jameson, GC.

Carl Schofield, GC.

energy and courage throughout, knowing all the time that his father was lying under the fall.' (LG 8th October 1940)

Thomas Jameson was born in Lancashire on 14th February 1898 and educated at St Thomas School, Ashton-in-Makerfield, near Wigan. Following his schooling, he attended Wigan Mining and Technical College, although he started work as a coal miner in 1912. He rose to become manager and then General Manager at several other collieries in Lancashire, Staffordshire and North Wales, being appointed Area General Manager for the National Coal Board in 1948 and Labour Relations Director for the Midlands National Coal Board in 1960. He retired in 1964.

Mr Jameson was married and had one daughter. His spare time interests included bowls, gardening and reading. He died, aged 82, on 29th March 1980 at Buckley, Clwyd, North Wales.

Carl Mallinson Schofield was born in St Helens, Merseyside, on 5th January 1902 and educated at Parr Flat Infant School and Alinson Street Council School in the town, until the age of 14, when he went to work at Southport Colliery. In addition to his daily work, he studied at night school at the Gamble Institute, to obtain his Under-Manager's Certificate. As this involved three full days a week, he worked night shifts as well.

He worked at a number of local collieries: Collins Green, Bold, St Helens and Clock Face, the latter until his retirement in 1963, early, owing to ill-health. During the war, he did Home Guard service.

Mr Schofield and his wife, Jane, had two daughters. His hobbies were car maintenance and trying to patent new ideas in mining machinery. He was awarded the Queen's Silver Jubilee Medal in 1977 and died on 9th January 1978. His Edward Medal is now in Plymouth Museum.

Thomas HULME, GC (formerly EM in Silver)

Thomas Hulme was born on 23rd October 1903 in Leigh, Lancashire and went to school at West Leigh St Paul's Church of England Elementary School until 1915, when he won a scholarship to Leigh Grammar School, staying there until 1921, when he went to Wigan Mining and Technical College part-time from 1921 to 1927. He worked in a variety of pits doing several different jobs, until retirement in 1967 as Area General Manager of St Helens and West Lancashire Area. He was Under-Manager of Parsonage Colliery in 1941 when he won the Edward Medal in Silver.

'On the 23rd January 1941, a fall of a roof took place above the coal face in a pit at the Parsonage Colliery, Leigh, Lancashire. Two hewers were trapped when the roof collapsed; one of them was quickly released but the other, Thomas Wignall, could not get away, and as the fall was continuing he was in an extremely dangerous position.

The only access to Wignall was along the conveyor belt over which the roof had squeezed down to two feet, and Mr Hulme the Manager of the colliery, crawled along

Thomas Hulme, EM, with his wife, Dorothy; Buckingham Palace, May 1941.

the belt, a distance of about six to eight feet, and, although he had to lie prone on the belt and there was the possibility of a total collapse of the roof at any moment, he stayed there for about one and a half hours. He succeeded in building three hard wood chocks round Wignall to prevent the roof closing down on him, and afterwards helped Wignall to get clear of the debris so that he could roll over on to the conveyor belt and crawl out, practically unhurt. During the whole of the rescue operations Hulme was in imminent danger. The roof was visibly and audibly moving about over him and there was constant dirt trickling; if the roof had collapsed he would almost certainly have been killed.

In rescuing Wignall, Hulme showed outstanding courage and saved Wignall's life at the risk of his own.' (LG 16th May 1941)

Thomas Hulme, GC.

Mr Hulme was invested with his Edward Medal on 27th May 1941. He is married and his wife, Dorothy, was awarded the MBE for work in the National Savings Voluntary Movement; she is also a Justice of the Peace. They have no children.

Thomas Hulme holds the Defence Medal and Queen's Silver Jubilee Medal 1977 and was awarded the rare Bronze Medallion by the Carnegie Hero Fund Trust. He presented his EM to the Leigh Town Silver Collection. As hobbies, he enjoys bee-keeping, amateur dramatics, music (piano) and gardening.

He now lives in quiet retirement on Merseyside.

Percy Barnard WELLER, GC (formerly EM)

Percy Barnard Weller was born on 6th June 1898 and went to Leigh Parish School, near Reigate in Surrey. Nothing is known of his early life. From 1916 until 1923 he served with the East Surrey Regiment, being awarded the British War and Victory Medals for service in the First World War. There follows a gap in our knowledge of his employment but by 1932, he was employed as a ganger at North Holmwood Brickyard in Dorking, Surrey and remained there, apart from the war years of 1939–45, when he worked at the Schermuly factory at Newdigate, Surrey. It was here he performed the act of courage which won for him the Edward Medal.

'On the 16th May 1941, an explosion accompanied by fire occurred in a certain building in which explosives were being broken down. A workman named Clark who was

163

Above: Percy Weller, EM, at Buckingham
Palace, with his wife and son, November 1941.
Inset: Percy Barnard Weller, GC.

employed in the building was badly
burned. Weller, another workman,
entered the burning building and succeeded in rescuing Clark, although the
rescued man died subsequently from
the effects of his injuries. In effecting this rescue Weller ran great personal risks not
only from the fire but also from the danger of a further explosion which did in fact occur
shortly afterwards, demolishing the building.

Weller showed outstanding courage in effecting the rescue of his workmate Clark in
most difficult and dangerous circumstances.' (LG 24th October 1941)

During the last war, Mr Weller served in the Home Guard, attaining the rank of Corporal.

He was married with two sons and two daughters and in 1977 received the Queen's Silver
Jubilee Medal. His hobbies were cricket and football.

He died on 22nd April 1979 and his Edward Medal was not surrendered for exchange,
although he elected to receive the George Cross in its place.

164

William Frederick BAXTER, GC (formerly EM)

William Frederick Baxter was born in Coventry on 22nd September 1907 the son of John and Emma (née Matthews). He was educated at Edgwick School, Coventry and on leaving, was employed at the Daimler Motor Company, Singer Motors and the Standard Motor Company. It was whilst an employee of the latter that he won the Edward Medal.

'On the 8th July 1941, an accident occurred in the Service Department of the Standard Motor Co Ltd, Coventry, in which an employee of the firm, named Ross, was trapped by the arms between the rope and pulley at the end of a 130-foot long lattice work jib of a crane, so that he was in imminent danger of bleeding to death or falling a distance of 110 feet to the ground. Baxter, another employee of the firm, after obtaining a rope and some first-aid dressings, climbed to the top of the jib where he lashed the man more securely, applied dressings and a tourniquet to his injuries and stayed with him for an hour until a rescue was effected by the Fire Brigade.

Baxter displayed great initiative and intelligence in collecting first-aid equipment and his action in applying the dressings and tourniquet in such perilous position was one of great gallantry. There is little doubt that but for his action Ross would have died either through loss of blood or by falling from the end of the crane to the ground.' (LG 1st May 1942)

It was as an employee of the Standard Motor Company that Mr Baxter joined the St John's Ambulance, a move which doubtless he found of considerable assistance during his rescue of

William Baxter, GC, at his reinvestiture with his family, daughter Shirley, wife Edna and son Gerard, November 1972.

165

Mr Ross. During the last war, William Baxter served with the ARP during the whole of the Coventry bombings.

He received the Certificate of the Carnegie Hero Fund Trust for his act, in addition to the Edward Medal.

Retiring in 1958, Mr Baxter now lives with his wife, Edna, in a 300-year-old cottage in Yorkshire. He is still active and enjoys reading, crosswords and walking. He has three children, ten grandchildren and six great-grandchildren.

He was awarded the Queen's Silver Jubilee Medal in 1977 and his Edward Medal was presented to the City of Coventry Museum.

Wilson Charles Geoffrey BALDWIN, GC (formerly EM)

Wilson Charles Geoffrey Baldwin was born in Dovercourt, Essex, on 9th April 1912. Nothing is known of his early life and education.

He won the Edward Medal in 1942 for courage after an explosion in a munitions factory.

'On the 20th November, 1942, a violent explosion occurred in a building in which explosives were being mixed, and resulted in the immediate death of the two occupants of the building, the complete destruction of the building itself, and considerable damage to adjacent structures. In one of these, a Nitrating House, a charge of 1,800 lb of nitroglycerine was in the pre-wash tank, and another nitration was about half completed. Although the building became filled with fumes and steam, the operator,

Dr Geoffrey Baldwin at his reinvestiture with his family, 1972.

166

Mr Wheeler, and his assistant, Mr Sallows, remained at their posts and took prompt steps to control the nitration and render the explosion harmless. They were assisted in this by Dr Baldwin, the Assistant Works Manager, who arrived on the scene shortly after the explosion. He noticed that about three square feet of wood above the pre-wash tank were smouldering vigorously and throwing off sparks. With Mr Wheeler's assistance he extinguished this very dangerous outbreak. The danger which these three men averted was a very real one since there is little doubt that if the necessary steps had not been taken, an explosion in the building would have occurred and that such an explosion occurring a few minutes after the first one when many workers had left their buildings and were in the neighbourhood would have caused a great number of casualties. All three men could probably have saved their lives by running, but they can have been under no illusion as to the danger they were in. They acted promptly and courageously, and without thought of their own safety in circumstances of considerable danger.' (LG 16th April 1943)

William Sallows and Frank Henry Wheeler also received the Edward Medal for this incident.

Dr Baldwin received the Bronze Medallion of the Carnegie Hero Fund Trust, in addition to the Edward Medal and he was awarded the Queen's Silver Jubilee Medal in 1977. He has been a member of the Executive Committee of the VC and GC Association for many years.

John WELLER, GC (formerly EM)

John Weller was born on 30th September 1912 and educated at Kirbymoorside, Yorkshire, Sprouson Grammar School, Lincoln and Downholme School, Richmond, Yorkshire. At some time, his mother remarried and his stepfather's name was Brown. For some reason, *The London Gazette* citation originally referred to him as John Weller Brown, a mistake perpetuated in a number of sources.

'When a violent explosion took place at an ammunition railhead Mr Weller was in a hut forty yards away. The hut collapsed and he was blown a considerable distance. The explosion was followed immediately be extensive fires in the surrounding area, caused mainly by grenades and incendiary bombs scattered from adjoining trucks. Mr Weller, though badly shaken, returned to the hut, which was already on fire. He was joined by another man, who,

John Weller, GC.

though injured himself, was able to assist him to extricate three other injured men from the ruins of the hut and to carry them to safety. They then assisted in the rescue of killed and injured from other burning and wrecked buildings. Mr Weller continued the work of rescue and fire fighting.

Mr Weller well knew that the area contained other loads of high explosives which might well have exploded. His behaviour showed courage, initiative and determination of a high order.' (LG 9th and 30th June 1944)

Mr Weller was a haulage contractor from 1935 to 1974. He and his wife, Rita, had one daughter and his spare time interests included darts, dominoes and dancing. In 1977, he was awarded the Queen's Silver Jubilee Medal and his Edward Medal was presented to Richmond Museum at the time of the exchanges.

He died in Richmond, Yorkshire, on 14th December 1978, aged 66.

Frank Emery NIX, GC (formerly EM)

Frank Emery Nix was born on 22nd April 1914. Nothing is known of his early life and schooling.

He won the Edward Medal for bravery in a mining accident in 1944 in the following circumstances:

Frank Nix, EM.

'On the 18th April at 4.30 am a "Bump" occurred at a coal face on which Mr Ernest Vickers and a workmate were cutting coal with a compressed air machine, as a result of which the flamper over the bars from the left side end of the machine was broken for a distance of thirty-five yards, the roof lowering about eight inches. The bar over Mr Vickers lowered under the weight of the flamper and pinned his head against the edge of the conveyor pans. Mr Vickers shouted and signalled by knocking on the pans, and his workmate stopped the machine to go to Mr Vickers' assistance, shouted to Mr Nix and then went round the roadways about 2,500 yards with another man to give what help he could.

Mr Nix had three men with him behind the machine, two of whom slid down the pans and placed a prop in order to take the weight off Mr Vickers' head. Mr Nix followed them down but seeing that nearly all the props within ten yards of the accident were broken, sent them back and himself went along to where Mr Vickers was trapped.

With the aid of the third man, Mr Nix worked his way down the face side, resetting broken props as necessary. By this time the roof had lowered to about fifteen inches from the floor, and this was consequently a most difficult job. The setting of about twelve props brought Mr Nix to a position about three yards from Mr Vickers, but owing to the fall of earth he was unable to see him. He went back to the machine to ascertain the position and then returned and began to clear away the earth with the assistance of one of the men. After Mr Vickers was exposed, it became obvious that the only way to liberate him without a further fall was to lighten the bar, and this he did by breaking the flamper with a hammer, working most carefully for fear of a further fall which would have involved not only Mr Vickers and himself but two of the other men as well. When the bar was sufficiently uncovered, Mr Nix sawed off the end and liberated Mr Vickers, who fortunately was suffering only from severe shock and bruises. The whole operation took about two hours during which Mr Nix was working in a height of about fifteen inches under a broken and detached roof, the confined space offering little chance if a further fall had occurred.' (LG 21st November 1944)

Mr Nix was subsequently employed with the National Coal Board as a Deputy with the Area Salvage Team. He received the Queen's Silver Jubilee Medal in 1977 and now lives in retirement in Derbyshire.

He declined to exchange his original insignia in 1971.

Henry Harwood FLINTOFF, GC (formerly EM)

Henry Harwood Flintoff was born in Yorkshire on 3rd September 1930, attending school at Low Mill, Farndale. He was a 13-year-old schoolboy when he won the Edward Medal for a most courageous rescue.

'On the 23rd June last, a farmer was driving a bull which turned on him, knocked him down, and knelt on his chest. Harwood Henry Flintoff [sic], a 13-year-old schoolboy who assists the farmer immediately left his work in a neighbouring field and ran to his aid. After a struggle with the savage bull, in which the farmer was injured, Henry Flintoff though unarmed caught hold of the animal and together he and the farmer managed to grasp the ring in the bull's nose, and to hold on to it until they both became exhausted. The bull then broke loose but was caught and led to its shed by a farm labourer who came

Henry Harwood Flintoff, GC.

169

to assist with a pitch fork. By his courageous action this boy saved the farmer from more serious injury and from possible death.' (LG 8th December 1944)

For his bravery, Mr Flintoff also received the Certificate of the Carnegie Hero Fund Trust. It appears that his parents were unaware of the incident until the press arrived at his home the next day and it was only on that day that Henry realised what had in fact happened. He says, 'I was not too robust – merely a puny six stone . . . I thank God for giving me the strength. For the rest of my life I shall continue to do so!'

From 1945 until 1972, he was employed in agriculture and from then until the present time, he has been a gardener. A bachelor, his hobbies are aircraft and aviation in general and vintage cars. He holds the Queen's Silver Jubilee Medal 1977 and his Edward Medal is now in the Rydale Folk Museum.

William WATERSON, GC (formerly EM)

William Waterson was born about 1904, although nothing is known of his early life and education. He was married and had one daughter.

He won the Edward Medal in 1945 whilst working for GEC.

'At 4.30am on Saturday the 18th August, 1945, two workmen employed in the carbon-black plant at the works of the General Electric Company Ltd, Birmingham, were engaged in collecting newly manufactured lamp black from a brick chamber. The men were unprotected and had to withstand a high temperature as well as an unpleasant atmosphere due to particles of oily lamp black, while carbon monoxide was present from burning soot. After a short time Webb, one of the workmen, collapsed and his companion, Albert Edward Stranks, being unable to move him, sought assistance. Breathing apparatus was stored at the works fire station some distance away; when Stranks called for help, the fire alarm was properly sounded. To await the arrival of breathing apparatus would inevitably have resulted in some delay and as the event conclusively proved, there was no time to lose. William Waterson, who was the first to arrive on the scene after the alarm was given, joined Stranks and in order to avoid any delay in going to Webb's assistance, without hesitation though fully realising the risk, entered the chamber and attempted to pull the man out. Webb was covered in sweat and carbon black and rescue work was difficult as it was not possible to get a proper grip on him. They were unsuccessful at first and on coming out Stranks collapsed; but Waterson continued to make attempts, entering four times in all. On his last entry he was accompanied by John Thomas Hewitt, a member of the works Fire Brigade, who had then arrived with a rope but not with the breathing apparatus; together they succeeded in bringing Webb out, who, unfortunately, was found to be dead.

The hazards were serious owing to the presence of the carbon monoxide gas, intense heat, complete darkness except for the light from a portable acetylene lamp (the carbon covered surroundings absorb all light and give no reflection), the deposit of carbon black and the confined space, conditions to which Waterson and Hewitt were unaccustomed.

Both Waterson and Stranks suffered badly from gassing and were removed to hospital, and Hewitt suffered to a lesser extent.' (LG 2nd April 1946)

Above: William Waterson, EM, receives his
Carnegie Trust awards. Inset: William
Waterson, GC.

The Carnegie Hero Fund Trust awarded
Mr Waterson their Certificate for this attempted rescue.

William Waterson died in Birmingham
on 24th March 1973 and his Edward Medal
is now in the Department of Archaeology,
Museum and Art Gallery, Birmingham.

Sydney BLACKBURN, GC (formerly EM)

Sydney Blackburn was born on 15th July 1908 but nothing is known of his early life and
schooling.

He won the Edward Medal in early 1947.

'An explosion occurred at Barnsley Main Colliery at about 12.15 pm on Wednesday the
7th May last. Harry Crummack, a Chargeman Filler, and Sydney Blackburn, Shot-
firer, were at the end of the face away from the resulting flame; Crummack was blown
over by a gust of wind caused by the explosion but quickly recovered and with
Blackburn, despite fumes and dust, assembled men who had scrambled from the face

and led them to a place of safety. Returning they found a number of injured men to whom they gave assistance and then proceeded through fumes and clouds of dust in search of others. Both men, while taking every reasonable precaution, continued to disregard their own personal safety in their efforts to ensure that none of the victims were left unattended in the danger area.' (LG 21st November 1947)

Harry Crummack was also awarded the Edward Medal.

Mr Blackburn, who still lives in Yorkshire, was awarded the Queen's Silver Jubilee Medal in 1977 and donated his Edward Medal to Leeds City Museum.

Sydney Blackburn, GC.

David BROWN, GC (formerly EM)

David Brown was born on 7th May 1900, near Edinburgh. He went to work in the shale mines in 1914 and remained there until the early 1960s, when the shale mines closed down.

He married Annie Anderson Cowan and they had three sons and two daughters.

Mr Brown was awarded the Edward Medal and the Carnegie Hero Fund Trust Certificate for the act of gallantry described below.

David Brown, EM, with his wife, Annie, in the 1950s.

David Brown, GC, at his home in the early 1970s.

'An explosion occurred in the Burngrange Shale Mine, West Calder, Midlothian, at about 8pm on Friday, 10th January 1947, when fifty-three persons were at work underground in the district. Firedamp was ignited by an open acetylene cap lamp and the initial explosion started fires which spread rapidly. David Brown, the Overman, descended the pit and proceeded with a fireman to explore the narrow workings where men were trapped. Though they encountered smoke for a time it was not sufficiently dense to prevent progress but as they passed the junction of another heading increasing smoke compelled their withdrawal. After waiting a few minutes Brown made another attempt, alone, to get inbye. He actually got into No 3 Dookhead, where he shouted but got no response. He saw no signs of the inbye men nor of their lights, and he was forced to withdraw again. On his way outbye, he again met the fireman, who said he had been trying to improve the atmospheric conditions in the inbye section by a partial opening of some brattice screen doors, but this step was of no avail. The atmospheric conditions were getting worse all the time, due to the spreading of the fires, the extent and seriousness of which even then were not generally realised. Brown, however, did realise the seriousness of the position in relation to the trapped men and immediately sent word explaining the position to the manager who was dealing with fires elsewhere, asking for all possible assistance and making it quite clear that there was no hope of undertaking further exploratory work without the use of rescue teams wearing self-contained breathing apparatus. He then set out to discover for himself where all the smoke was coming from.

Although the National Fire Service was never intended for firefighting underground in mines, nevertheless, a team at once volunteered for this duty. Two members of the team donned their one-hour Proto-Breathing Apparatus. Underground, they met the Overman, Brown, who pleaded for the use of the two sets of Proto-Apparatus, so that he and another trained member of the Burngrange Mines Rescue Team could make another attempt to get into the workings beyond No 2 Dook. Using the one-hour apparatus borrowed from the NFS Brown and his companion made an unsuccessful attempt to rescue the trapped men. At 11.15pm under the captaincy of Brown a fresh team wearing goggles and using a life-line again attempted to reach the men but were forced to return as the temperature was very high and the smoke so dense that their lights could not be seen. There had been a fall of stone and sounds of strata movement were heard. A further attempt along another level led to the discovery of another fire and it became certain that there was no hope of saving the men until this was under control. The work of fire-fighting continued for four days and it was not until the night of 13th/14th January, that it was considered practicable to send a rescue team beyond the fire area. With one exception the bodies of all the fifteen men who lost their lives by the effect of afterdamp and fumes were in No 3 Dook.' (LG 13th January 1948)

David Brown enjoyed walking, outdoor activities and being with his family. He retired to West Calder and died there on 1st December 1977, having received the Queen's Silver Jubilee Medal a few months before. His EM is now on display in West Calder Comprehensive School.

John Daniel CHARLTON, GC (formerly EM)

John Daniel Charlton was born on 24th December 1895 and went to school at Hetton. He became a coal miner in 1909 and retired as a Deputy in 1960.

He received the Edward Medal for the gallant but vain rescue in 1947 of John Kirkhouse.

John Daniel Charlton, EM, displays his Edward Medal.

'On the 30th March 1947, a repairer employed at Hylton Colliery, Durham had been overcome by gas in an old disused road. Deputy Charlton was informed that the man was missing and at once conducted a search, testing for gas with his flame safety lamp. He had gone only a few yards when he found gas present, at the same time noticing ahead of him, some thirty yards from the entrance, a light from an electric lamp. Accompanied by another man he went towards the light but owing to gas had to return. Assisted now by Austin and many other men Charlton endeavoured to clear the air by erecting bratticing across the air intake and extending it down the middle of the road; he coupled air hosing to the compressed air range, but when used this had little effect and the rescuers could get no nearer than twelve yards from the man. Despite the conditions Charlton and Austin, crawling on their knees and at times on their stomachs succeeded in reaching the man who was then alive but unconscious. Whilst dragging him out Charlton was slightly overcome and had to have a short rest, but soon returned to help Austin who in turn collapsed for a time, and was dragged clear. Others finally assisted Charlton to carry the man to fresh air; and it is unfortunate that although given artificial respiration for a long period he failed to respond.' (LG 10th February 1948)

John William Austin was also awarded the Edward Medal for his part in this rescue.

Jack Charlton also received the Carnegie Hero Fund Trust Certificate.

Sadly, Mr Charlton's wife, Sara Jane, died a few days before the announcement of the award of the EM.

He had two sons and two daughters and his hobby was horses and horse racing. He died at Sunderland, Tyne and Wear, on 25th February 1976, aged 81. His Edward Medal is now in the Sunderland Museum and Art Gallery.

William Younger, GC (left, rear), and three colleagues bringing out an injured man from the Louisa Colliery disaster, 1947.

John HUTCHINSON, GC (formerly EM in Silver)
Harry ROBINSON, GC (formerly EM in Silver)
Joseph SHANLEY, GC (formerly EM in Silver)
William YOUNGER, GC (formerly EM in Silver)

'Shortly before midnight on the 22nd August 1947, a serious explosion of fire damp and coal dust occurred in the Louisa Old Section of Louisa Colliery, Durham. William Younger, Joseph Shanley and Harry Robinson, Deputies, who with an intimate knowledge of the main roads and ventilating circuits of the mine could have made their way quite easily to safety, went instantly to the scene of the disaster, where they were soon joined by John Hutchinson, Overman, who came down from the surface. Twenty-four persons, all of whom were incapacitated either by injuries or carbon monoxide poisoning were in the district at the time. Nineteen of them died and but for the prompt and continuous heroic work performed by Younger, Shanley, Robinson and Hutchinson, who voluntarily faced conditions of acute danger for a period of $1\frac{1}{2}$ hours, there can be little doubt that not one would have survived.

The circumstances and conditions would have tested the courage and endurance of the bravest and strongest. The atmosphere was so thick that the beams of the cap lamps could penetrate only a foot or so which meant that the rescuers could do nothing to guard against danger from falls of ground, a very real danger after an explosion, and the road in places was almost completely blocked by tubs derailed by blast.

Five of the injured were brought out alive from the affected workings; two of them died later in hospital and three recovered.' (LG 20th July 1948)

John Hutchinson was born on 25th July 1907 in County Durham and attended Oxhill Council School. On leaving school he became a miner and worked in the pits for forty-five years.

He received the Certificate of the Carnegie Hero Fund Trust for his rescue work mentioned above.

Mr Hutchinson was married but there were no children of the union. His spare time interests were tennis and golf. His Edward Medal went to Beamish Museum, County Durham and he died at Stanley, County Durham, on 9th June 1975, aged 67.

Harry Robinson was born in the mining village of New Kyo, near Stanley, County Durham, on 27th December 1916 and went to school locally, leaving at age 14.

He started work at the Morrison South Pit in 1931 as a pony driver. Both his father and his brother worked at this pit. Later, in 1935, he transferred to Busty Pit but could not settle there, so in 1937, after his father had had a fatal accident the previous year, he returned to South Pit.

Mr Robinson and his wife, Mary, were married in 1941 after a three-year courtship and they have a son and two grandchildren.

He started Deputy work in 1942 and in the same year trained on the mines rescue team, for which he holds the Bronze (5 years), Silver (10 years) and Gold (15 years) Medals.

In 1945, after closure of South Pit, Mr Robinson was transferred to Louisa Pit and later the same year, was sent to the Morrison Pit as a rescue man but it was in the Louisa Pit that he was to win his Edward Medal in Silver, along with three colleagues, as detailed above.

By January 1974, Harry Robinson had worked in the pits for forty-two years and decided to retire. He and his wife spend summers in their caravan on the North East Coast and take continental holidays in the winter. In his younger days, he enjoyed breeding fowl of a number of types and also, during the last war, pigs.

He declined to exchange his Edward Medal and offers the following insight into the reason. His own words are used, with minor editorial amendments: 'I got the EM in Silver in 1948, presented by King George VI. In 1971, I could have changed it for the GC. The EM I could put in any museum of my choice. But my wife and our son said, "No. The EM was the medal you got for the work you did, so keep it. You could not have said the GC was the medal you got." So that is why I have the EM in Silver.'

Mr Robinson was awarded the Queen's Silver Jubilee Medal 1977 and now lives quietly in County Durham.

Joseph Shanley was born on 8th January 1907 in County Durham and went to school at St Joseph's RC School, Stanley, County Durham. On leaving school in 1921, aged 14, he was a miner until 1936, when he became a Deputy. He was one of the four men to be decorated for bravery at the Louisa Pit disaster.

He and his wife, Ethel, had two children, a son and a daughter, and his spare time interests were gardening, reading and membership of the St John's Ambulance Brigade.

Left to right: Joseph Shanley, Harry Robinson, William Younger and John Hutchinson receive their Carnegie Trust Certificates.

John Hutchinson, GC, with his family at Buckingham Palace.

Harry Robinson, GC, and his wife at Christmas 1983.

Joseph Shanley, GC, presents his Edward Medal to Retford Mining Museum.

William Younger, GC, talks to Princess Alexandra, 1981.

In common with his three colleagues, he received the Certificate of the Carnegie Hero Fund Trust and was awarded the Queen's Silver Jubilee Medal in 1977.

He died on 23rd April 1980 at Rainworth, Nottinghamshire, aged 73 and his Edward Medal is now on display at Lound Village Hall Mining Museum, near Retford, Nottinghamshire.

William Younger was born on 24th March 1909 in County Durham and went to school at South Moor. He spent forty-six years as a coal miner, commencing in 1923 and retiring in 1969.

As detailed above, he was one of the heroes of the Louisa Pit disaster in 1947, for which he received the Edward Medal in Silver, which is now in Beamish Museum, County Durham.

Mr Younger is a widower and has one child. During the war, he was in a reserved occupation but has been a member of the St John's Ambulance Brigade for many years, holding their medal with two bars for long service. He is also a Serving Brother of the Order of St John of Jerusalem and was awarded the Queen's Silver Jubilee Medal in 1977.

He now lives quietly in County Durham.

Walter Holroyd LEE, GC (formerly EM)

Walter Holroyd Lee was born on 29th May 1919 in Yorkshire. After leaving school, he became a miner in 1944, remaining in this employment until retirement in 1978.

He won the Edward Medal in 1947 for gallantry in saving a coleague's life.

Walter Holroyd Lee, GC.

'A fall of roof occurred at about 4 pm on the 11th November 1947, at Wombwell Main Colliery, near Sheffield, burying three men. The first rescuer on the scene was a workman, George Dorling, whose calls for assistance attracted a coal cutter team of three men. Dorling had climbed over the fall in an attempt to reach the trapped workmen and was being followed by the cuttermen when the roof again began to move and a second fall occurred. The cuttermen were just able to withdraw in time but Dorling could not escape and was killed instantly. Shortly afterwards Walter Holroyd Lee arrived on the scene when it was clear from their cries that two of the men trapped by the original fall were still alive. Lee then took the lead in making a way through the fall and after some two hours one of the men was extricated alive. Lee was largely instrumental in saving this man's life and exposed himself to great risks in so doing.' (LG 10th May 1949)

George Dorling was posthumously awarded the Edward Medal for his courage.

Mr Lee and his wife, Elsie, had four daughters and a son.

In 1977, he was awarded the Queen's Silver Jubilee Medal and he died in Barnsley on 24th May 1984, five days short of his 65th birthday. His Edward Medal is now in Cushworth Park Museum, Doncaster.

Charles WILCOX, GC (formerly EM)

Charles Wilcox was born on 11th May 1919 and educated at Osler Street School, Ladywood and Raddleburn Road School, Selly Oak, both in Birmingham. Employed as a painter and decorator by Birmingham Corporation from 1933 to 1939 and 1946 to 1965, it was in this capacity that he won the Edward Medal.

'On Tuesday, 23rd August 1949, Mr Charles Wilcox (aged 30), a painter employed by Birmingham Corporation was engaged with other men in painting a Council House building in the centre of the city.

One of the other painters, Alfred Leslie Burrows (aged 21) mounted a ladder to begin painting an exterior window on the third floor of the building, and at the top of the ladder, about forty-five feet above the street, climbed on to an arched sill about eighteen inches in width which was sited below the window. He then found that the window was

Charles Wilcox, GC, with his family at Buckingham Palace.

A very rare and interesting photograph of an act resulting in a gallantry award. Charles Wilcox winning the Edward Medal in Birmingham in 1949.

bricked up from the inside and that there was nothing for him to hold to enable him to retain his balance. He turned round to return to the ladder but could not see it, became frightened, and crouched down to retain his balance on the ledge.

The foreman painter saw Burrows' predicament and sent another painter to his assistance but this man returned to the ground after supporting Burrows for a few minutes. Charles Wilcox then climbed the ladder to assist Burrows and by kneeling on a flat piece of masonry, some eighteen inches square, at the end of the arch was able to support the other man who was suffering from severe shock. Mr Wilcox stayed in this position for forty-five minutes until the Fire Brigade arrived and Burrows who had become unconscious was brought to the ground, by a fireman, in a safety belt which Wilcox strapped upon him.

During the period that Mr Wilcox was on the ledge with Burrows he was in considerable danger of falling had the other man kicked out or made any violent movement.' (LG 30th September 1949)

The accompanying illustration is an exceedingly rare instance of a photographic record of an act of gallantry resulting in a decoration.

During the war, Mr Wilcox served as a Private with the South Staffordshire Regiment, earning the 1939–45 Star, Africa Star, Burma Star, Defence and War Medals. He was awarded the Queen's Silver Jubilee Medal in 1977.

Mr Wilcox is married with three children – two daughters and a son – and his hobbies are gardening, carpentry and restoring old clocks.

He was a car assembler from 1965 to 1980 but had to retire on medical grounds. He still lives in Birmingham and presented his Edward Medal to the City of Birmingham Museum and Art Gallery.

Thomas George MANWARING, GC (formerly EM)

Thomas George Manwaring was born on 11th December 1916. Nothing is known of his early life and schooling.

He is one of the last three living recipients to be awarded the Edward Medal and the only one to exchange it for the George Cross. The circumstances are as follows:

'On the 30th June, 1949, the Arthur and Edward Colliery, Forest of Dean, was flooded by a sudden inrush of water.

Evacuation of the mine was ordered as soon as the water broke in, and the escape of the men who were underground was greatly helped by Frank Bradley, a man of 63, who took charge of the man-riding trolleys which ran up and down the long steep main road leading to the shaft, and helped the escaping men to travel swiftly over part of their road to safety.

After many men had been helped in this way another official advised Bradley to escape at once, telling him that the rising flood would soon cut off the main shaft. Bradley, however, refused to leave the pit, saying that some of his men were still underground. He thereupon walked back into the inner working of the mine. At this point it should be emphasised that Bradley acted deliberately and without rashness, although he knew that once he was cut off from the main shaft he would have to stay

182

below ground for a long time and that he might never reach the surface again. As an official of the mine he must have known also that blackdamp (carbon dioxide) was given off in the mine and that the stopping of ventilation by the flood made accumulations of this suffocating gas likely. He must also have known that there was an incalculable danger to be expected from the disturbance to roof supports caused by the flood.

While Bradley was helping with the evacuation another official of the mine, Oswald George Simmonds was showing great calmness in the face of danger. He went round his district ordering his men out of the pit and telling them how to reach the main shaft safely through the flooding roads. When he was himself about to leave he heard that two men, one old and feeble, were still left in the workings. He immediately returned to help them. When he found them, they were with a third man, Thomas George Manwaring, who had voluntarily stayed back to help them.

Simmonds and Manwaring, helping and sometimes carrying the old men along with them, made their way towards the main shaft, meeting Bradley on the way. At the first opportunity they telephoned to the surface and were told that the flood had cut them off completely from the main shaft, but that they might be able to reach a second shaft through the workings of the mine.

Bradley, Simmonds and Manwaring set off, taking with them the other two men, of whom one was practically exhausted. The way to the second shaft was very hard, and the air in places very bad. The men had in some places to wade through torrents of water, and in others had to clamber over falls of ground. They never, however, abandoned their weaker comrades, one of whom at times was so exhausted that he had to be pushed along in a truck.

Eventually, after spending nearly seven hours underground, struggling through the flooded mine, the party reached the second shaft and were hauled to safety.' (LG 1st November 1949)

Frank Bradley received the Edward Medal in Silver and Oswald George Simmonds the Edward Medal for this brave rescue.

Thomas Manwaring now lives in quiet retirement in Gloucestershire, although unfortunately he still suffers from the effects of his experience underground in 1949. He received the Queen's Silver Jubilee Medal in 1977 and donated his Edward Medal to the City Museum, Gloucester.

A BRIEF HISTORY OF THE VICTORIA CROSS AND GEORGE CROSS ASSOCIATION

Although various suggestions had been put forward about forming a VC Association, it was not until after the Centenary Celebrations in 1956 that such an Association was finally founded. Prior to this, there had only been one occasion, in 1929, when VC, AM and EM holders had assembled as a company, the guest of honour being the Prince of Wales (later King Edward VIII).

The 1956 Centenary gathered 299 VCs from all over the world, the focal point being a review of holders in Hyde Park by Her Majesty the Queen on 26th June. Other events included a party at Marlborough House, attended by Her Majesty Queen Elizabeth, the Queen Mother; a Thanksgiving Service in Westminster Abbey, when the Address was given by the Archbishop of Canterbury; and Receptions at the Guildhall and in Westminster Hall by HM Government.

With a large proportion of surviving holders meeting together in London over several days, there was discussion of forming a permanent Association and Sir John Smyth, Bt, VC, MC, at that time a Member of Parliament, agreed to be the founder Chairman.

A Committee was formed and aims were agreed:

(a) To establish a central focus and headquarters in London for Victoria Cross holders from all over the world, and to provide a centre where holders could meet and communicate.

(b) To cement the brotherhood of the holders of the Victoria Cross throughout the Commonwealth and thereby, through our own unity and strength, make some contribution towards the maintenance of world peace.

(c) To give such help and guidance to one another as might be possible from time to time.

The Royal Society of St George, which had done much to help the War Office in organising the Centenary, made all VC holders Honorary Members.

At the second Committee meeting, it was decided to invite George Cross holders to become Associate Members; this was felt to be in accord with King George VI's direction that the George Cross (awarded for gallantry when not in direct personal contact with the enemy) should be of equal standing with the Victoria Cross. It was also felt that future awards of the George Cross were likely to be rather more frequent than the Victoria Cross, since warfare on the scale of the last two wars could not be visualised. In 1961, it was decided it would be more appropriate for GC holders to be full members, and the Association was renamed 'The Victoria Cross and George Cross Association'.

Reunions have taken place in the summer of alternate years since 1956, save for a slight readjustment to enable a reunion to take place during Silver Jubilee year – 1977. In 1958, it was apparent that a number of holders could not afford to travel to London, so the then Minister of Defence (Mr Duncan Sandys) sought and obtained Government approval for

A delightful study of the senior and junior surviving Albert Medallists, Thomas McCormack and Margaret Purves, July 1969.

travel warrants and subsistence to be given to those in the UK who would otherwise be unable to attend. Since 1968, the RAF have been able to make some adjustment in their flight schedules to enable overseas members and their relatives to travel to the UK at minimum expense, many of whom would not otherwise have been able to attend. The RCAF have made similar arrangements for Canadian members and their relatives. Some national and commercial airlines have also been most helpful.

In 1962, with funds drawn largely from the donations of well-wishers, a VC and GC Benevolent Fund was formed and with this Fund, the Association has been able to give a helping hand to members in need; more particularly the Association puts members in touch with organisations such as the Royal British Legion or individual Service or Regimental charities who are able to determine and meet their needs. The Association is aware that among holders of the George Cross are those who have never served in the Armed Forces and therefore lack this help, having only the Social Services to approach for assistance. Fortunately, though, a substantial donation was given several years ago to be used primarily for George Cross holders and the Association is able in some way to fulfil this requirement. On the death of a VC or GC holder, immediate assistance can be given to a widow, if so required.

In October 1971, Her Majesty the Queen directed that all holders of the Albert Medal and the Edward Medal should become holders of the George Cross and might exchange their insignia for the George Cross, if they so wished. The Association welcomed these ladies and gentlemen to their company and many attended the 1972 reunion, giving an even greater and wholly delightful variety to the membership.

It is inevitable, with members scattered widely in Britain and overseas, that keeping in touch is difficult; but the reunions, lasting a few days rather than compressed into one single event, give members the opportunity to make and maintain lasting friendships for the sharing of problems as well as happiness into the future.

Over the years, reunion events have variously included receptions given by Her Majesty the Queen, the Prime Minister and at the House of Lords; a Service of Remembrance and Rededication at St Martin-in-the-Fields, the Members' Reunion Dinner, and visits to Hampton Court, Greenwich and the Royal Tournament. In November 1985, for the first time, one VC holder and one GC holder represented the Association at the annual Festival of Remembrance at the Royal Albert Hall.

Her Majesty the Queen graciously consented to be the Patron of the Association in 1957, and Sir Winston Churchill became the first President in 1959. After Sir Winston's death in 1965, Sir John Smyth, Bt, VC, MC, was elected President and continued to hold the office of Chairman as well, until 1971, when Rear-Admiral B. C. G. Place, VC, CB, DSC, was elected to the latter office. Sir John Smyth died in 1983 and Her Majesty Queen Elizabeth the Queen Mother graciously consented to become President, with the Rt Hon Lord de l'Isle, VC, KG, GCMG, GCVO, as Deputy President.

There are now 160 members in the Association, comprised of 60 holders of the Victoria Cross and 100 holders of the George Cross; 34 VC members and 27 GC members reside overseas.

The Victoria Cross and George Cross Association
Room 04
Archway Block South
Old Admiralty Building
Whitehall
London SW1A 2BE

Telephone 01-930 3506

THE ALBERT MEDAL ASSOCIATION

Like the Victoria Cross Association, the Albert Medal Association was formed in the centenary year of the decoration, although recruitment had begun the previous year. Fifteen holders of the medal assembled for the first time on 17th June 1966 in London.

The motivating force behind the formation of the Albert Medal Association was the fact that the decoration had become obsolescent from the end of 1949, when the King had decided that it would no longer be awarded in Gold and only posthumously in Bronze. It therefore followed that it must become defunct at some time in the future and it was felt that such a fate should not befall the country's most prestigious award for gallantry – the George Cross and George Medal notwithstanding.

It should be noted that no brief was ever held for the Edward Medal, despite the fact that the holders of that decoration also eventually benefitted from the exchanges, though there were from time to time some 'unofficial' contacts. However, there was never an Edward Medal Association.

As early as 22nd July 1965, it had been proposed in the House of Lords by the Marquis of Ailesbury that Albert Medal recipients should be allowed to exchange their awards for the George Cross, in a similar manner to recipients of the Empire Gallantry Medal (which was the cause of all the concern) but the Earl of Longford rejected the suggestion on behalf of the Government.

Nothing daunted, the Association and individual members of it continued to press their cause and were rewarded by an announcement in the House of Commons on 14th November 1968 by the Prime Minister that holders of the Albert and Edward Medals would henceforth receive an annuity of £100 per annum, non-taxable.

As related in the chapters on the Albert and Edward Medals, the situation was finally resolved – not, it must be said, to everybody's satisfaction at the time – by revoking both medals by Royal Warrant and re-investing the surviving recipients with the George Cross.

The final meeting of the Albert Medal Association, which, of course, was integrated into the Victoria Cross and George Cross Association, took place in July 1972. During the six years of the Association's life, seventy-three members were enrolled. Six of these were ladies, fourteen lived overseas; one held the Albert Medal in Gold but he died on 13th August 1969. The average age was over seventy and awards ranged over the years 1908 to 1949. Death kept the maximum membership to fifty-eight. Twenty-three persons who had inherited the Albert Medal, i.e. the next of kin of those who were deceased, were enrolled as Associate Members and gave considerable support.

Thus, it will be seen that the Albert Medal Association was formed for entirely different reasons to the Victoria Cross Association. The man who did most to orchestrate the campaign to restore the Albert Medal recipients to their rightful status was the late Instructor-Commander David Evans, GC, MA, BSc, RN (Retired), who died as this book was being compiled. He had been trying to have some permanent record made of the surviving Albert Medal holders and their deeds ever since the winding up of the Association he had done so much to help. This work is really a tribute to him and it is fitting that he should have the last word:

'In retrospect, it seems strange that important changes concerning a Royal award of eighty-three years' standing could be made without legal authority and continue unchallenged for seventeen years, and that it should take a further six years of constant pressure by leading members of a democracy and a change of Government to produce an acceptable and legalised solution to the problems so created.

It was unfortunate that the Association's activity had to be mainly political, especially when it had become obvious that success must inevitably mean the demise not only of the Association but also of the decoration which it had set out to restore; yet it seems better that its life should have been brought to an honourable close than that it should pass unheeded into the limbo of forgotten things. Queen Victoria had designed the Albert Medal herself as a memorial and so it remained for over a century, and now many Albert Medals will be preserved in museums and schools as a permanent reminder of a great Queen and her Consort and of their leadership in a proud period of British history. The former wearers are now members of the most honourable Society in the world, the Victoria Cross and George Cross Association which knows no distinction of class, creed, race.'

BIBLIOGRAPHY

An Unknown Few by Phillip P. O'Shea. P. D. Hasselberg, Government Printer, Wellington, New Zealand, 1981.

British Gallantry Awards by P. E. Abbott and J. M. A. Tamplin. Nimrod Dix, 1981.

Gallantry by Sir Arnold Wilson, MP, and Captain J. H. F. McEwen, MP. Oxford University Press, 1939.

The Journal of the Orders and Medals Research Society (various).

The Register of the George Cross. This England, 1985.

The Register of the Victoria Cross. This England, 1981.

They Dared Mightily by L. Wigmore and B. Harding. Australian War Memorial, Canberra, ACT, 1963.

Various magazine and newspaper articles.

ACKNOWLEDGEMENTS

Grateful thanks are extended to the following for assisting with the provision of material and photographs:

Diana Birch, MA.
Michael Blackburn, Esq.
Mrs Nora Buzzell.
Wing Commander F. G. Carroll, RAF (Retired).
Syd Cauveren, Esq.
Miss Rose E. B. Coombs, MBE.
Major A. F. Flatow, TD.
Major J. M. A. Tamplin, TD.
Ken Williams, Esq.
Mike Willis, Esq.
This England.
The Victoria Cross and George Cross Association.
The Imperial War Museum (The late Canon Lummis Collection).
HMSO (for *London Gazettes*)

And especially the holders of both decorations and relatives of deceased recipients, without whom this work would not have been possible.

INDEXES

VICTORIA CROSS

(P) indicates a posthumous award.

GEORGE CROSS (direct awards)

(P) indicates a posthumous award.

GEORGE CROSS (formerly Albert Medallists)

	London Gazette	
Abbot, E. G.	12 Mar 20	29
*Abbott, G. F. P.	14 Dec 17	58
Allen, Miss F. A.	19 Nov 35	73
*Armytage, R. W.	3 Aug 28	69
Ashburnham, Miss D.	21 Dec 17	31
Bagot, A. G.	20 Aug 18	45
Bastian, G. L.	17 Aug 43	91
Brown, R. L.	4 Jan 18	34
Bryson, O. C.	11 Jan 18	36
*Buckle, H.	27 Apr 20	60
Butson, A. R. C.	28 Sep 48	95
Cannon, H.	26 Apr 18	42
Chalmers, J.	7 Jul 22	61
Cleall, W.	30 Dec 19	57
Cowley, J. G.	19 Nov 35	75
Davis, T. N.	26 Mar 18	40
Day, H. M. A.	7 Jan 19	49
Ellis, B. G.	18 Jul 19	44
Evans, D. H.	31 Jan 19	53
*Fairclough, J.	8 May 28	67
Farrow, K.	15 Oct 48	101
Feetham, C.	18 Mar 19	55
Ford, A.	21 Aug 17	28
Fraser, Miss H. E.	31 Jan 19	51
*Gibbons, J. E.	11 Aug 42	84
Gibbs, S.	8 Feb 27	63
*Goad, W.	26 Jan 43	86
*Gregson, J. S.	2 Feb 43	86
Harwood, H. S.	19 May 16	27

Hawkins, E.	29 Jun 43	89
*Hay, D. G. M.	8 Jul 41	82
Howarth, A.	2 Sep 41	83
Hutchison, A.	4 Jan 18	35
Kavanaugh, R. M.	17 Oct 30	72
Keogh, M. S.	14 Jan & 19 May 16	26
*Knowlton, R. J.	14 Dec 17	29
Lowe, A. R.	8 Feb 49	103
Lynch, J.	15 Jun 48	98
McAloney, W. S.	18 Feb 38	78
McCarthy, W. H. D.	27 Jul 43	91
McCormack, T. W.	23 Jul 09	25
Maxwell-Hyslop, A. H.	19 Nov 29	71
May, P. R. S.	25 Nov 47	94
Miles, A.	29 Apr 41	80
Mitchell, J. H.	29 Apr 41	81
Newman, A. W.	5 Mar 18	38
*Oliver, D.	3 Aug 28	69
Rackham, G.	3 Jan 19	48
Reeves, J. A.	25 May 43	87
*Rhoades, W. E.	1 Jan 18	33
Richards, R. W.	6 Jul 23	62
*Ridling, R. G.	9 Dec 19	56
Riley, G.	3 Oct 44	93
Robertson, P. D.	18 Jun 18	37
Smith, G. S. Bain	30 Sep 27	64
Spoors, R. G.	19 Nov 35	76
*Stanners, J. G.	21 May 18	43
Vaughan, Miss M.	1 Nov 49	104
Walker, C. H.	15 Dec 42	85
*Walton, E. W. K.	8 Jun 48	97

*Watson, V. A.	8 Mar 18	39
Western, D. C.	13 Aug 48	100
Williams, S.	30 Aug 18	47
Wolsey, Miss H. E.	28 Mar & 26 May 11	26

*Elected to retain their original insignia.

GEORGE CROSS (formerly Edward Medallists)

London Gazette

Allport, E.	30 Sep 32	135
*Baker, J. T.	22 Nov 29	125
Baldwin, W. C. G.	16 Apr 43	166
Baster, N.	17 Apr 36	143
Baxter, W. F.	8 Jul 42	165
Beaman, G. W.	17 Apr 36	143
Blackburn, S.	21 Nov 47	171
Booker, D. N.	4 Feb 38	147
Booker, S.	4 Feb 38	147
Brown, D.	13 Jan 48	172
Charlton, J. D.	10 Feb 48	174
Clarke, A.	5 Aug 38	149
Craig, B.	1 Jun 23	114
Crosby, B. F.	15 May 28	124
Darker, R. E.	30 Sep 32	135
Dixon, J.	23 Feb 40	156
Edwards, A. F.	22 Jan 18	109
Fisher, B.	15 Aug 39	155
Fletcher, D.	26 Jan 26	120
Flintoff, H. H.	8 Dec 44	169
Gough, J. I.	17 Jun 30	130
Haller, F.	20 Jan 39	153
*Harris, C. T.	22 Jan 18	109

Havercroft, P. R.	22 Jun 17	109
*Heslop, G. C.	26 May 36	146
Hulme, T.	16 May 41	162
Hutchinson, J.	20 Jul 48	175
Jameson, T.	8 Oct 40	160
Johnston, J.	19 Mar 26	122
*Jones, B. L.	9 Sep 38	150
Kent, E. W.	20 Dec 38	151
King, R. H.	20 Oct 31	132
Lee, W. H.	10 May 49	179
Little, R. S.	5 May 39	154
Lloyd, W.	9 Dec 27	123
Locke, G.	2 Mar 26	121
McCabe, J.	13 Jun 19	112
Manwaring, T. G.	1 Nov 49	182
Meadows, A. J.	29 Dec 31	134
Morris, A. E.	4 Jul 24	115
*Nix, F. E.	21 Nov 44	168
Pearson, R.	20 Oct 25	119
Pollitt, J.	17 Apr 36	143
Purvis, J. S.	22 Nov 29	125
*Robinson, H.	20 Jul 48	175
Saunders, R. B.	8 Oct 37	147
Schofield, C. M.	8 Oct 40	160
Shanley, J.	20 Jul 48	175
Shepherd, J. W. H.	14 Feb 30	127
Smith, C.	28 Jun 40	157
Soulsby, O.	30 Sep 32	135
Sykes, F.	30 Sep 32	135
Temperley, S. J.	30 Sep 32	135
*Thomas, A. D.	31 Mar 31	131

Thomas, T.	6 Feb 34	142
*Thompson, M.	28 Jun 40	157
Tyler, A.	14 Feb 30	128
Wastie, G. C.	6 Jun 30	129
Waterson, W.	2 Apr 46	170
Weller, J.	9 Jun 44	167
Weller, P. B.	24 Oct 41	163
*Whitehead, T. A.	5 Sep 22	112
Wilcox, C.	30 Sep 49	180
Williams, O.	29 Nov 32	140
Wilson, H.	22 Aug 24	117
Yates, P. W.	30 Sep 32	135
Young, A.	1 Jan 17	111
Younger, W.	20 Jul 48	175

Names appearing in bold type relate to the Edward Medal in Silver.
*Elected to retain their original insignia.